DATA STRUCTURES & ALGORITHMS

INTERVIEW QUESTIONS
YOU'LL MOST LIKELY BE ASKED

277

Interview Questions

VIBRANT
PUBLISHERS

Data Structures And Algorithms
Interview Questions
You'll Most Likely Be Asked

ISBN-10: 1-946383-06-6
ISBN-13: 978-1-946383-06-8

Library of Congress Control Number: 2011921388

Vibrant Publishers books are available at special quantity discount for sales promotions, or for use in corporate training programs. For more information please write to **bulkorders@vibrantpublishers.com**

Please email feedback / corrections (technical, grammatical or spelling) to **spellerrors@vibrantpublishers.com**

To access the complete catalogue of Vibrant Publishers, visit **www.vibrantpublishers.com**

Table of Contents

Data Structures

Algorithms

This page is intentionally left blank

Data Structures And Algorithms

Review these typical interview questions and think about how you would answer them. Read the answers listed; you will find best possible answers along with strategies and suggestions.

This page is intentionally left blank.

Data Structures

This page is intentionally left blank.

Chapter 1

General Concepts Of Data Structures

1: What are Data Structures?

Answer:

Data Structures are a method of structured or organized data storage which is easier to manage. Data usually has 2 aspects – the definition and its implementation. Data structures make sure they keep both the aspects separate. The definition is made available for different implementations for different programs or usages. A data structure, as the name suggests, stores the information in a structured way so that it can be easily created, viewed and managed. This involves creating complex data types which are a combination of various basic data types. One example can be a customer data type which will have a CustomerId of type Integer, Customer Name of type String and Address of type String.

2: What are the advantages of using Data Structures?

Answer:

Data structures help store the information in a structured way. This makes data storage and retrieval much easier than the conventional sequential storage. Data structures keep the data away from its implementation. This involves Data abstraction and encapsulation which are very important for code efficiency. Not only data, their relation can also be stored in data structures. One efficient way of implementing data structures are the databases. Data structures are also used for indexing data.

3: What is a data object?

Answer:

Data objects are the entities that actually contain the information. Data objects are the implementation of the data structures defined by the programmer. Data objects can access the methods and information stored in the data structure to store, process and retrieve information. It can be of type a complex structure or an array or an object in object oriented programming. A data object exists in the computer's memory till it is garbage collected whereas the data structure is accessed only when the object is being created. In simple terms, data structure is the data definition while data objects are its implementations.

4: What are data types?

Answer:

Data types define what kind of information is stored in a variable or data member. There are primitive data types such as integer, character and Boolean and there are complex data types such as arrays data structures. Most of the programming languages require the variables to be declared before they are accessed. This helps in memory allocation depending on the data type of the variable. For example, an integer data type may require 4 bytes of memory while a float may require 8 bytes, depending on the programming language used. Complex data types are made of two or more primitive data types combined.

5: What are the different types of Data Structures?

Answer:

Data Structures can be categorized in many ways, though broadly, they can be categorized as Non-Linear and Linear data structures. Linear data structures are those that are sequential, like lists, arrays, stacks and queues. They are stored and can be accessed sequentially. Non-Linear data structures are objects or information that is not stored in an order. Graphs and trees are best example of non-linear data structures. While sequential data is easier to manage, non-linear data is not so easy. But many real-time solutions require non-linear data structures to be implemented such as hierarchical data, geographical positioning and games.

6: Explain the Linear Data Structures.

Answer:

When information is stored in a sequential manner, it is easy to store and manage. Data structures, stored in an order or sequentially, are called linear data structures. Arrays, Lists, Queue, Stack, and even files are stored sequentially. While arrays and other data structures can be accessed directly with the position marker, files are accessed sequentially. Arrays can be single dimensional or multi-dimensional. But they are stored sequentially in the memory. For example, if there is an array of numbers num[5] = {2, 5, 7, 6, 1} it is stored sequentially in the memory as

Num

(Position) 0	1	2	3	4
(Value) 2	5	7	6	1

This makes sure that linear data structures can be created and managed using pointers.

7: Explain the non-linear data structures.

Answer:

Non-linear information implies that the information does not follow a specific pattern for storage. But they can be related in other ways. Hierarchical information such as tree pattern or geographical information that depends on positions can never be sequential. But they can be relative. Non-linear data structures are supported by most of the programming languages for implementing graphics, images, global positioning, location mapping and inheritance. These concepts are crucial to represent many real-time entities while developing applications and programs.

8: What are the basic operations possible in Data Structures?
Answer:
Every data structure allows some basic operations such as inserting, deleting, updating, traversing, searching, and sorting. Insert operations can be allowed in the beginning, end or the middle of the data structure based on the type of data structure. Similarly, deletion can also be allowed in the beginning, end or the middle of the data structure. Even though some data structures such as stacks and queues are very strict about inserting and deleting information, traversing and sorting the data structures work more or less similarly for all. Traversing and sorting are possible only because the data is stored sequentially.

9: What is a node?
Answer:
A node is the basic form of data structure. It basically consists of a member variable which holds the value and the address of the next node. The address part will be null for the last element

of the data structure. A node will allow all the basic operations of a data structure since the address to the next data node is stored in each node. With pointers, these dynamically allocated nodes can be easily accessed and traversed through for effecting the various operations such as insertion, deletion, updating, and sorting. An array is built by linking the nodes with the address element. There can be 2 addresses in a node where one address points to the previous node and the other address points to the next node.

10: What are Primitive Data types?

Answer:

Data types provide more information about the data. Most of the programs allow creating new data types which are implemented as enumerations and the values become the constants in the program. This makes the program more readable and understandable. For example, if you create a new data type for weekday with allowed values Sunday, Monday, Tuesday, Wednesday, Thursday, Friday and Saturday, these values are treated as constants instead of using switches or if-else constructs to check the value. Standard Primitive data types allowed in most of the languages are integer, character, Boolean, real and set. Integer data type allows storing number values ranging between negative and positive depending on the programming language. Real type allows storage of a subset of real numbers. Boolean allows true and false values. Char typically allows all alphabets, space, and a few special characters depending on the language used.

11: Explain the record structure.

Answer:

A set of related information can be stored as a record. It can be considered as a complex data structure stored sequentially. While the different elements of each entity are stored in columns, one entity comprises of a record. For example, the information regarding a student can be considered as the data structure and each student's detail can be considered as a record.

Type Student {

    StudName String;

    StudId int;

    DateOfBirth date;

    StudSex char;

    StudMaritalStatus char;

}

When you collect the student information, it will be stored in the following manner

Structure - Record No	Stud Name	Stud Id	DateOfBirth DD/MM/YYYY	StudSex M / F	StudMaritalStatus S / M / W / D
1	Smith Allen	1	10/9/1982	M	S
2	Mary Lynda	2	09/02/1982	F	M
3	Alex George	3	20/01/1983	M	S

The information regarding each student is stored as a record. Records make data storage and retrieval much easier to manage.

12: What is a file? How is it different from a record?

Answer:

Files store data sequentially in the hard disk. Every information that we want to store permanently or make persistent is stored as a named file in the hard disk or in a database as records. The main difference between files and database are that files store information sequentially while the records are stored as structured information. A file will have the same data type information stored. But the record will have multiple data types as defined in the data structure. The length of a file can be dynamically allocated, based on the storage memory available on the disk or allotted to a particular user. For records, each record will have the maximum size allocated as per its definition that comprises of different data types.

13: Explain the difference between sequential and structured data.

Answer:

Sequential data is easier to create but difficult to manage. Structured data is complex to create and manage but is the best when it comes to retrieval and processing. Sequential data can be considered as text files with no structure and structured data can be considered as data in tabular form or as records as we get from the database. While text information is easier to create, retrieving specific information is very difficult with sequential data. The entire file has to be loaded and specific search has to be performed to retrieve which will scan through the entire file. With structured data, it can be considered as information in tabular form. Specific columns or rows can be spotted and easily retrieved which makes data retrieval more efficient. But creating and managing structured data requires experienced professionals.

14: Explain the different sorting methods commonly used to sort arrays.

Answer:

Sorting the information available is an important aspect of data processing. Sorting is nothing but rearranging the information available in a particular order. When it comes to arrays, sorting the information can be done in many ways. The commonly used techniques to sort an array are insertion sort, bubble sort, selection sort, quick sort, tree sort, merge sort, and shell sort. Each sorting method has its own logic and algorithm and involves rearranging the array elements in the ascending or descending order. While some sorting techniques involve rearranging every element of the array during the process, some techniques use methods to find the lowest first and position it and consider the rest of the array during each pass.

15: Explain Selection sort.

Answer:

In Selection sort, the basic idea is to find the smallest number and position it in the first array index and then move ahead for the next one and position it in the second and so on till all the elements are refilled. This is if you want to sort in ascending order. If you want to order in descending order, start with the biggest number first. Find the following example, if you have an array with 5 elements and want to sort it in ascending order:

Original Array -> 5, 3, 1, 9, 2

1st pass -> 1, 3, 5, 9, 2

2nd Pass -> 1, 2, 5, 9, 3

3rd Pass -> 1, 2, 5, 9, 3

4th Pass -> 1, 2, 3, 9, 5

5th Pass -> 1, 2, 3, 5, 9 – which is the final sorted array.

16: Explain Bubble sort.

Answer:

Bubble sort works with swapping the adjacent array elements. It takes longer time as the array gets longer since for each pass, all the adjacent elements have to be checked and swapped if necessary. For an array with 5 elements and want to bubble sort it in ascending order:

Original Array -> 5, 3, 1, 9, 2

1st pass ->

5, 3, 1, 9, 2 -> 3, 5, 1, 9, 2 -> 3, 1, 5, 9, 2 -> 3, 1, 5, 9, 2 -> 3, 1, 5, 2, 9

2nd pass ->

3, 1, 5, 2, 9 -> 1, 3, 5, 2, 9 -> 1, 3, 5, 2, 9 -> 1, 3, 2, 5, 9 -> 1, 3, 2, 5, 9

3rd Pass ->

1, 3, 2, 5, 9 -> 1, 3, 2, 5, 9 -> 1, 2, 3, 5, 9 -> 1, 2, 3, 5, 9 -> 1, 2, 3, 5, 9

If selection sort required 5 passes, bubble sort got completed in 3rd pass. In each pass, the largest number became the last element and the next one, the next largest and so on.

17: What are linked lists?

Answer:

A linked list is a collection of connected nodes. Each node will have a data element and the address that links to the next node. The first node will have no data. It will only have the link to the next node. The last node will have only data and the link to the next node will be null. The first node is called the head and the last node is the tail. Linked lists help the programmer to dynamically create arrays. There are 3 types of linked lists – singly-linked, doubly-linked and circular-linked list. The singly-linked list will have only one link in each node that points to the next node. The doubly-linked list will have the links or the pointers to the previous node and next node. The circular-linked list will have the last node pointing to the first node's address of the linked list. It can be singly or doubly linked.

18: Explain Binary Search Tree.

Answer:

Binary Search Trees will have a root with 2 nodes attached. The nodes can be sub-trees or simply nodes. The left side nodes will have values less than the root and the right side nodes will have values greater than the root. There can be balanced and unbalanced binary trees. The balanced trees are when each node has either no sub-node or has 2 sub-nodes. Unbalanced binary trees are when a node has only one sub-node either to its left or right.

19: Explain the different algorithm patterns used with data structures.

Answer:

Data Structures form the key element of programming for all programmers. One needs to understand some basic algorithms commonly used with data structures which will help handling all types of complex data objects. Since data structures can be implemented in different ways in different programs, understanding the basic algorithms will help implement them better in real-time situations. Graph algorithms help a programmer handle Graph related data easily. Dynamic programming algorithms help in dynamic allocation of memory for arrays and other data objects. Searching and sorting algorithms are required everywhere. Applying the various number theories and various mathematical formulas such as prime factorization, factorials etc. will help creating applications involving complex mathematical equations.

Geometrical and network algorithms help in establishing complex networks easily.

20: What are the practical applications of data structures?

Answer:

Data structures are the basic idea behind many complex software solutions that. The concept of data structures are used in building operating systems, numerical analysis, database management system, graphics, artificial intelligence, statistical analysis applications, compiler design and simulations. For example, memory allocations use the heap and stack concepts to store and retrieve information in the computer memory. Any business application that requires complex matrices and graphs will require the implementation of data structures. The database is the basic requirement for most of the business applications as it stores a large amount of structured data which is easier to process and retrieve.

This page is intentionally left blank.

Chapter 2

Arrays

21: What is an Array?

Answer:

An array is a set of values represented by a single variable. Arrays are usually stored sequentially which makes it possible to access each element by its index. An array will have a fixed number of elements that are accessible with their index. An array can store any type of data as allowed by the programming language or the platform used. You can have integer arrays or string arrays and even arrays of objects and structures. The maximum number of elements allowed in an array is mentioned in the array declaration so that the memory can be allocated together. This makes sure that the array elements are sequentially accessible using the index or pointer dynamically. In some languages like C, a string is represented by a character array.

Ex: int arr[5] = {2, 4, 6, 8, 10};

char alphabets[10] = {'a', 'b', 'c', 'x', 'y', 'z', '1', '2', 'h', 'i'};

string names[3] = {"Smitha", "Allen", "Ritik"};

22: What are the basic operations possible with Arrays?

Answer:

All arrays are implementation of data structures and hence allow most of the operations allowed in them. The following operations are possible in Arrays:

a) **Insert** – You can insert an element into an array provided, the array does not overflow. You can access the index and insert into that position.

b) **Update** – You can update the existing values of an array using the index number.

c) **Delete** – You can delete the existing values of an array using the index number.

d) **Traverse** – You can access and print each element of an array using the index number sequentially.

e) **Search** – You can search through the elements of an array by using the value or index to search.

23: How you insert into an Array?

Answer:

When you are trying to insert an element into a particular position in an unordered array, you need to push the elements next to it to the next position and insert the new value in the specified position. For example, in the array 3, 4, 6, 7, 9 if you want to insert 5 in the 3rd position, you have to do the following steps

a) First start from the last position and move it to the next position till you reach the 3rd position.

b) 9 has to move to the 6th position

c) 7 has to move to 5th position and

d) 6 has to move to 4th position

e) Then you can insert 5 at the 3rd position.

Now the array will be 3, 4, 5, 6, 7, 9.

24: How do you delete from an Array?

Answer:

When you delete an element from the middle of the array, you have to rearrange the rest of the elements to occupy the position just before it. If you want to delete 6 from the array 3, 4, 5, 6, 7, 9, you have to take the following steps.

a) You have to delete the 4rd element in the 3rd index.

b) Go to the next element, 4th index and move it to 3rd index - 3, 4, 5, 7, 7, 9

c) Go to the next element, 5th index and move it to 4th index - 3, 4, 5, 6, 9, 9

d) Go to the currently 6th element and make it null since null marks the end of array - 3, 4, 5, 6, 9, null

e) Since that's the last element, your delete is complete and now your array looks like this 3, 4, 5, 6, 9.

25: Explain the search operation in an Array.

Answer:

Array can be searched based on value or index. Searching an array on index is simple, you can directly access the value at the index with array[*index*]. When you are searching for value in an array, you have to search the array till you find the value in it. If the array has n elements, you have to carry on with the search till you find the element or you reach the (n-1)th index which is the last element of the array. You can do this using a loop statement which breaks the loop when the value is found in the array. You can search the value of at the end of the loop and if n is equal to the size of the array, the value is not found in the array.

26: What is an iterator?

Answer:

Iterator is basically a variable or object used to traverse through a list or an array. While some programming languages such as Java contain an iterator object, in other languages, a pointer is used instead. An iterator will have 2 basic functions – to reference an element of the array at the given position and to move to the next position as required by the program. Iterators can be implicit or explicit. Implicit iterators are when the program traverses the array for each element in the array without worrying about the index or position. Explicit iterator uses the position or index of the array to point to a particular element and has to be directed to the next element.

27: What is a matrix?

Answer:

A Matrix is a 2 dimensional array that stores data in a structured way. It has rows and columns in which it stores the information. Each element can be accessed using the combination of row and column index. Matrices are used for many purposes. The database tables can be considered as a matrix implementation since information is stored in rows and columns. Each row is a record and each column contains specific information. A Matrix is also used to represent graphs since it contains information in rows and columns. Each matrix element will have 3 components – the row index, the column index and the value in it.

This page is intentionally left blank.

Chapter 3

Stacks

28: Why are stacks used to perform recursion?

Answer:

A Recursive function will call itself repeatedly. It is important to know who called the function with what value so that accordingly it will return the value to the right caller. Stacks function in the concept of LIFO or Last In First Out. For the same reason, it will recognize the last caller of the function that called it and will return the corresponding value to it. Recursion usually functions by stacking the caller addresses in the order in which the function is called. Hence, it is important to use a separate stack every time the recursive function is called explicitly in the program. For example, if factorial(n) is a recursive function which is called twice in a program, for each call, a separate stack should be used. To be more specific, in the same program that calls factorial(x) and factorial(y), separate stacks should be used.

29: What are the basic stack operations?

Answer:

Stacks follow the concept of Last In First Out. This implements that only the last element is always accessible in the stack. Stacks usually permit the following operations:

a) **Push** – The Push operation pushes an element into the stack. Stacks allow insert into the last position available

b) **Swap** – Swaps the two topmost elements

c) **Rotate** – Rotates the topmost elements in the stack

d) **Pop** – Removes the last element in the stack

e) **Peek** – Peek retrieves the last element in the stack without popping or removing it.

30: Can you implement a queue using a stack? Explain

Answer:

Stack follows the Last In First Out method while Queue follows the First In First Out method. To implement a queue using stack, we will need 2 stacks. Stack 1 is used to pushing elements in or to insert the elements and stack 2 is used for popping them out. When Stack 2 gets empty from popping out the elements, all the elements in stack 1 are emptied into stack 2 in reverse order. This implements the LIFO method for effecting FIFO based queue.

Stack 1

a	b	c	d	
0	1	2	3	4

Stack 2

f	g	h	i	j
0	1	2	3	4

The next element to be inserted will be pushed into the 4th index of Stack 1 and the next element popped out will be j from Stack 2. Then i, h, g and f will be popped out in the same order. Once Stack 2 is empty, the elements of Stack 1 is inserted into stack 2 in the order d, c, b, a. So what went in first, 'a', will pop out first.

31: Write the basic algorithm to implement the push function for a stack

Answer:

The Push operation is used to insert an element on to the top of a stack. To insert an element into a stack, first the current last position has to be checked for overflow. If the maximum size allowed for the stack has run out, you have to exit the program. If otherwise, find the last element's address and increment the pointer to move to the next position and insert the element there. Now this position will be considered as the top of the stack. To insert the next element or for the next push, the same steps are repeated.

32: Explain the steps involved in the Pop operation for stack.

Answer:

The Pop operation retrieves and removes the lastly inserted element from the stack. This is comparatively easier to implement. First of all, the stack is checked whether it has some value or is empty. If it is empty, there's nothing to pop out and the same is informed to the user. If the stack is not empty, the last position is located and the element is deleted. The position pointer is rolled back to the previous position to indicate that it is the last element of the stack.

4	5	
3	4	4
2	3	3
1	2	2
0	1	1
Index Position	Original Stack	Popped Stack

33: Explain three practical applications of Stacks in software.

Answer:

Stacks are extensively used for memory management. If you take most of the programming languages and platforms, memory management depends on stacks. That's one reason you may have come across *Stack Overflow* error in Java and C. Most of the programs use stacks for managing the function call, parameters and other programming requirements. If your program requires some kind of backtracking to be done, you can implement stacks for the same. The undo / redo option available in MS Office is one example for stack implementation. Syntax parsing and expression evaluation also uses the stack implementation. Even compilers use the stack implementation to parse the code. The concept of stack is so basic and simple that it is used in many places in real-time implementation of various software and business logics.

34: What do you mean by stack overflow?

Answer:

When the user tries to push values into an already full stack, the system is unable to handle the process and throws a stack overflow error. Every stack is defined with a limited memory allocation. When the program dynamically tries to fill the stack beyond this allocated memory limit the stack overflows. Even if the stack memory is dynamically allocated, certain programming errors may cause stack overflow such as very deep or infinite recursion and large stack variables requiring large amount of memory. In these cases, when the memory is exhausted, stack overflow is affected. Another possible stack overflow situation is multi-threading where both the threads lock each other infinitely.

This page is intentionally left blank.

Chapter 4

Queues

35: What are the basic features of a Queue?

Answer:

Queues implement data structures that follow the First In First Out concept. What is inserted first comes out first. This means that push operation happens at one end of the queue while pop operation happens at the other end. Even though the queue and stack operations are similar, in contrast to a stack which is open only at one end, the queue is open at both the ends.

Stack (LIFO)

Push ->

g	f	e	D	c	b	a

Pop <-

Queue (FIFO)

Push ->

g	f	e	D	c	b	a

Pop ->

36: What are the applications of queue?

Answer:

While stacks are used in memory management, queues are used for buffering. When you want to print a number of documents, you pass the print requests to the print queue which buffers and prints the first print request first. Another implementation of queues can be used in transport system where the first come first served or first scheduled trip starts first has to be implemented. Queues are also used when you have to prioritize the tasks. The tasks with maximum priority are pushed in and popped out first. CPU tasks and interrupts are implemented as queue system, that is, FIFO. Another practical implementation is in call centers where the first received calls have to be answered first.

37: Explain how to implement a queue using an array.

Answer:

Every queue has a head and a tail. The head is the first element of the queue from where elements have to be popped out. Tail is the last element of the queue where elements can be pushed in. We can easily implement a queue using an array. In an empty queue, the head and tail will be the same element. As new elements are inserted into the queue, the tail is pushed to the next space available, to store more values and to denote the last element. As elements are popped out, the head is pushed to the next address to denote that the first element is released and the next element is the current first element.

38: What is a circular queue?

Answer:

In a circular queue, the head and the tail are connected to each other making it form a circle. Circular linked lists are implemented using circular queues. The tail and the head pointers of the circular queue will point towards the head of the queue. But since both are defined, it still follows the FIFO principle. Data is pushed into the head and popped out of the tail. Circular queues are used to define ring buffers.

39: Explain the steps involved in Enqueue operation.

Answer:

The Enqueue operation lets you insert new elements into a queue.

The operation basically consists of inserting an element to the back of the queue and move the rear or tail pointer one step forward to change its position to include the new element. The basic steps to follow for an enqueue operation are:

a) Find out if the queue has space

b) You cannot insert into a queue which is already full

c) If it does have space, increment the tail pointer to point to the next available space

d) Insert the value into the newly made available space

e) Now the tail will point to this newly added space.

Enqueue operation does not hinder the head pointer of a queue.

40: Explain the steps involved in dequeue operation.

Answer:

Dequeue operation is used to pop out or remove a value from the queue. Since the queue follows the principle of First In First Out, the head has to be considered to pop out the values. The following steps are taken for dequeue operation:

a) Find out if the queue has some value or not

b) You cannot dequeue an empty queue

c) If the queue has some value, move to the head of the queue from where the value has to be popped out.

d) Take the value out and increment the head pointer to point to the next position in the queue

e) Now that becomes the new head or the first element of the queue.

Dequeue operation does not hinder the tail pointer of a queue.

Chapter 5

Lists

41: What are the advantages of Linked Lists?

Answer:

Linked lists are a sequence of nodes connected to each other by a link to the next and or previous node. Linked lists are used to implement many real-time application requirements. One basic application of linked list is to create arrays dynamically. Since the linked lists contain the memory address to the next node, it need not be sequentially allocated. Each node will contain the address to the next node using which you can move to the next node. Linked lists allow easier implementation of stacks and queues. You implement insert and delete operations easily with linked lists.

42: List out the disadvantages of linked lists.

Answer:

While Linked lists allow dynamic implementation of arrays, they also come with many disadvantages. One main disadvantage is that linked lists take up additional memory since it stores the address to the next node or the pointer to the next node. Another issue with a linked list is that, none of the elements can be randomly accessed. It has to be sequentially accessed by traversing through each node to get the address of the next node. When it comes to singly linked list, there's no way you can move to the previous node or element.

43: What are the different types of linked lists?

Answer:

There are basically three types of Linked Lists.

a) **Singly Linked List** – These contain at least 2 parts for each node – one part contains the value and the other part contains the pointer to the next node. The last element's pointer of the singly linked list will be null.

b) **Doubly Linked List** – These contain at least 3 parts for each node – the value part, pointer to the previous node and pointer to the next node. The first element's pointer to the previous node will be null and the last element's pointer to the next node will be null.

c) **Circular Linked List** – When the last element's pointer points to the first element's address, the Linked List becomes circular.

44: Explain a singly linked list. What are its applications?

Answer:

A linked list which allows only forward navigation is a singly linked list. Each node of a singly linked list contains data as well as the address of the next node. One can traverse the singly linked list by following the next pointers till the next pointer becomes *null* at the end of the linked list. Singly linked lists are used to implement stacks, queues and dynamic arrays. They are used when only forward navigation is required and when the element's exact position or index is not known. The concept of linked lists is used whenever a random list of elements is to be accessed.

45: Explain a doubly linked list. What are its applications?

Answer:

A doubly linked list allows both forward and backward navigation since the nodes contain data along with the address of the previous node and the address of the next node. One can traverse forward and backward through the doubly linked list. The previous address of the first node will be null and the next address of the last node will be null in a doubly linked list. Doubly linked lists are used when arrays or the data structures need to be traversed in either direction, forward and backward. One main disadvantage of doubly linked lists is that they occupy more memory since 2 pointers are to be stored.

46: What is a circular linked list? What are its applications?

Answer:

A linked list becomes circular when its last node points to the head of the list. It can be singly linked or doubly linked lists. The basic idea is to set the address of the next pointer to point to the head or first element of the list. In case of a doubly linked list, the previous node of the first element points to the address of the last node of the list. The operating system works its memory like a circular linked list. Each program is a part of the linked list and is given a fixed amount of time and then moves on to the next program. This keeps running like a circle till all the applications are closed. Circular queues and multiplayer games are also implemented in the same concept as the Circular linked list.

47: How to find the length of a linked list?

Answer:

Iteration is the clue to finding the length of a linked list. You can use a counter variable that increments as the loop traverses through the linked list. Traversing is done checking for the next pointer till it becomes null. A counter is declared outside the loop and set to 0. A flag is declared outside the loop and set to true. The loop is a do while (flag) loop inside which the counter is incremented and the pointer is directed to the next address. When the next pointer is found null, the flag is set to false inside the loop. So as the counter increments and we traverse through the linked list, when the next pointer becomes null, or the last node is reached, the flag is set to false and we exit the loop. As we exit the loop, the counter is checked and that's the length of the linked list. The same logic can be applied using a recursive function also. Instead of the loop and flag, the function can be called recursively till the next is not null.

48: Explain the insertion operation in a singly linked list.

Answer:

While inserting into a singly linked list, the current node's next pointer will be null. But you have to point the previous pointer to the newly created node. The header will always point to the first node. And the tail node's next will be null. To every time you insert into a singly linked list, take the header's next address and store it in a temp variable tempAddress. Once the new node is created and memory is allocated, take its address and assign to the header's next. The address in the tempAddress will be the current node's next which will now point to the 2nd node.

Before Insertion –

Head->next = Node1

Node1->data = 30, Node1->next = node2

Node2->data = 20, Node2->next = node3

Node3->data = 10, Node3->next = null

After Insertion -

Head->next = NewNode1

NewNode1->data = 45, NewNode1->next = node1

Node1->data = 30, Node1->next = node2

Node2->data = 20, Node2->next = node3

Node3->data = 10, Node3->next = null

49: Explain deletion operation in a singly linked list.

Answer:

When you delete a node from the linked list, one point to note is to make sure the link to the next node is not lost. When you are deleting the last node, this is easy since all that's need to be done is to make the next pointer of the last but one node to null. Since the next pointer is lost, the linked list is considered to end there. To effect this, the following steps are taken:

Step 1: First find out the node to be deleted. While traversing, keep the next pointer of each node in a temp variable tempPrev, which should be available in the next iteration.

Step 2: Store the next-> pointer of the node to be deleted in another temp pointer tempNext.

Step 3: Move to the previous pointer using the address stored in the temp pointer tempPrev.

Step 4: Make the next point to tempNext which makes sure that the node to be deleted is no longer accessible by address within the linked list.

This logic works for all nodes, unless there's only one node which has to be deleted. In that case, the next pointer of the first node itself will be null and you can just make the linked list *null.*

50: How to bubble sort a linked list?

Answer:

Bubble sort involves looping and swapping. There are 2 loops required; the outer loop works num − 1 times if num is the number of array elements. The inner loop also works as many times. Once inside the inner loop, the checking and swapping is done. The inner loop makes sure that each element is checked against the next one for each pass. The outer loop makes sure that as many passes are done so that all the elements are fully sorted. To implement this for a linked list which is dynamic, we have to utilize some pointers and flags since we cannot depend on array counters and index. So for the outer loop the flag is the check point and the inner loop continues till it reaches the end of the linked list. Swapping is basically the same, if the current value is greater than the next value, swap them. The swapped flag is set to false or 0 once inside the outer loop. Every time the swap happens, inside the inner loop, the swapped flag is set to 1 or true. So for a particular pass, if there's no swapping done, it means that the linked list is ordered and swapped remains 0 and the loop exits.

51: How to insert into a doubly linked list?

Answer:

Each programming language will have its own syntax for

implementing and inserting into a doubly linked list. The basic steps to follow are:

Step 1: Declare a Struct with 2 pointers Prev and Next and the data element

Step 2: Have a temp pointer of type same as the struct and set it to null

Step 3: Within a loop

First Node

a) Check if the temp is null, then it is the first node.

b) Allocate memory for the struct to the temp so that it can be incremented based on the size required.

c) For the first node, set the prev and next pointers to Null

d) Accept the Value to be stored and store it in the linked list node

e) Point another temp pointer tempPtr to point to this node

f) Have yet another temp pointer tempPtr2 to point to tempPtr

The last 2 steps will be useful for the next nodes.

Other Nodes

a) Allocate memory for the struct to the temp so that it can be incremented based on the size required.

b) Set the prev and next pointers to Null

c) Accept the Value to be stored and store it in the linked list node

d) Make the next of this node to the tempPtr we assigned previously

e) Make the prev of tempPtr address to temp

f) And Point temp pointer tempPtr to point to this node

These last 3 steps make sure that the prev and next pointers address to the right nodes.

Step 4: Exit the loop when you are done entering values into the linked list

Step 5: Have a loop to display the values input. You will see that the values are displayed in the reverse order, in LIFO.

52: Write a C program to insert into a circular singly linked list.

Answer:

The Program will be as follows:

```
#include<stdio.h>
#include<stdlib.h>


//Defined a Circular Linked List
struct circularLL
{
    int dataVar;
    struct circularLL *nextPtr;
};
```

```
int counter = 0;
struct circularLL *nodePtr,*startPtr,*ptrTemp,*newLLPtr;


//Function to Create a Circular Linked List
void createCircularLL(struct circularLL *nodePtr){
    char charVar;
    startPtr -> nextPtr = NULL;
    nodePtr = startPtr;

    printf("\n Enter 'e' to Exit :");
    charVar = getchar();
    while(charVar!='e')
    {
        nodePtr -> nextPtr = (struct circularLL *) malloc(
        sizeof(struct circularLL));

        nodePtr = nodePtr -> nextPtr;

        printf("\n Enter a Number Value :");
        scanf("%d", &nodePtr->dataVar);
        nodePtr -> nextPtr = startPtr;

        counter++;

        printf("\n Enter 'e' to Exit :");
        charVar = getchar();
    }
}
```

```
//Function to Insert into a Circular Linked List
void insertCircularLL(struct circularLL *nodePtr)
{

    nodePtr = startPtr->nextPtr;

    ptrTemp = startPtr;

    newLLPtr = ( struct circularLL *) malloc( sizeof(struct
    circularLL));

    printf("\n Input 1st Node Value :");

    scanf("%d",&newLLPtr -> dataVar);

    ptrTemp -> nextPtr = newLLPtr;

    newLLPtr -> nextPtr = nodePtr;
}


//Function to Display a Circular Linked List
void displayCircularLL(struct circularLL *nodePtr)
{

    int countNum;

    nodePtr = startPtr -> nextPtr;

    countNum = counter;


    while(countNum)
    {
    printf("\n%d",nodePtr -> dataVar);

    nodePtr = nodePtr -> nextPtr;

    countNum--;

    }
}
```

```
int main()
{
    char charVar;

    createCircularLL(nodePtr);
    insertCircularLL(nodePtr);

    printf("List Items Are:\n");
    displayCircularLL(nodePtr);
    charVar = getchar();

    return 0;
}
```

53: Explain traversing through a linked list.

Answer:

Traversing through a linked list is very simple. Pointer arithmetic is the base for it. To start with, you need a pointer that points to the first position of the linked list. Simply assigning the linked list to the pointer will make sure that the pointer address is set to the beginning of the list. Create a loop that runs till the pointer is null. The pointer becomes null when it reaches the end of the linked list. Within the loop, for each address of the linked list, access the value stored there and you can do all types of processing or display the data. The last statement of the loop must be to access the next address which is stored in the *next* element of the same node. Assign the *next* address to the pointer and the loop continues till it becomes null at the end of the linked list.

```
ptr = linkedList
while ptr != null
    var = ptr->val
    <Any processing to be done>
    Print var
    ptr = ptr->next
end loop
```

54: What are the differences between a linked list and an array?

Answer:

The first and foremost difference between an array and a linked list is that array can be accessed randomly, while the linked list has to be accessed sequentially. While in arrays the array index is used to access an element, in linked list, a pointer is used to locate an element. Arrays are stored continuously in the memory while the linked list can be stored in any way since they are accessed using the address. For the same reason, arrays take more time for insertion, updating and deleting while in linked list these operations are easier. Arrays are static while linked lists are dynamic. One array element is not connected to another one with links or addresses, but the linked list elements are inter-connected with links. Arrays need less space when compared to linked lists that require additional space to store the pointers.

55: Consider a linked list with the following data: arrTrial

| B | D | J | L | E | C | A |

What will start->next->next->data yield, if start = arrTrial?

Answer:

The result will be J. Since start is arrTrial, the pointer is on the address of the first element of the linked list, which is B. Start->next goes into the address of D and start->next->next reaches the address of J. start->next->next->data will yield J since the data in the given address is J.

Chapter 6

Hash Data Structures

56: What is a hashing?

Answer:

Hashing is converting a set of key-value pairs into indexed information or array which is easier to handle and retrieve. The information is always stored in key-value pairs with an index supporting a faster search. The size of the hash table is used for hashing the index. Hashing is done by method of the *key* % size where *key* is the key of a particular element in the key-value pair and the *size* is the size of the hash table. It is basically mapping where a particular item is stored in the hash table.

57: What is a hash table?

Answer:

A hash table is like a collection of elements, where each value is stored in a slot. The mapping between a particular value of a hash table and its location or the slot in which it is stored is determined by a hash function. A hash table of size n will have $n - 1$ slots. The slot in which each element is stored is calculated using the modulo or % operator and the size of the hash table. If you have a hash table of size 5, the slots will be:

Values of the hash table – 9, 3, 5

Slot

0	1	2	3	4
5			3	9

Value

58: What is linear probing?

Answer:

Linear probing is the method in which collision resolution is done during hashing. When there is more than one value in the collection which results in the same address slot after hashing, the situation is known as collision since there are many elements trying to occupy the same address or slot while there are empty slots in the hash table. One method used to solve collision is by relocating the newer values into the next available empty slot. This requires scanning of the entire hash table and sometimes the next available slot might be the previous slot which is arrived only in the end. This method is called linear probing.

59: What are the common uses of hash tables?

Answer:

Hash tables store data in key-value pairs and are indexed. Indexing makes searches faster and hence, hash tables are used when there's a large volume of key-value pairs to be stored which has to be easier to search. Hash tables also lets you work around the four basic functions of collections – put, which works with a set of key, value pair and get, contains and remove that works with a key. Caching is a common usage that implements hash tables in the real time. Sometimes hash tables also let you store relational data without disturbing the original objects.

60: How do you use the right hash function?

Answer:

There's no hard and fast rule or stipulation as to how you can choose the right hash function. There are certain common traits observed in certain methods that perform optimally. These are not rules but can be considered as guidelines that can be followed in most of the cases. Clustering or collision is a common issue observed in hash functions and that has to be avoided at any cost. A higher probability of collisions will degrade the hash table's performance. A universal hash function is recommended when you want to ensure speed, simplicity, and performance. Purely additive hash functions tend to be collision-prone and hence need to be avoided. A uniform distribution of hash values is preferred in most cases.

61: Explain Collision resolution.

Answer:

Collision occurs when more than one hash value tries to occupy the same slot in a hash table. Usually, during collision, the next available empty slot is allocated the current hash value and it can be done in many ways. Chaining, open addressing, coalesced hashing, perfect hashing and probabilistic hashing are the common methods used for collision resolution. Chaining implements a linked list. Open addressing is done with linear or quadratic probing or double hashing. Open addressing basically works based on space usage. Coalesced hashing is a perfect combination of chaining and open addressing. Perfect hashing is effected when there's no collision. Probabilistic hashing method uses a bit array concept for hashing.

62: Explain Chaining.

Answer:

Chaining is one of the popular collision resolution techniques in which each slot which has more than one element allocated because of collision, is assigned a linked list with all the elements that collided into the same slot. It is one of the simplest and most efficient methods for collision resolution. Inserting into the hash table and deleting from it is very simple when using the chaining method. Chaining handles the performance factor of the hash table more gracefully. A chained hash table will inherit all the advantages and disadvantages of a linked list. Dynamic arrays can also be used instead of linked lists in chains.

63: Explain Open addressing.

Answer:

Open address hashing involves finding the next available slot to store the record instead of colliding slot. It can be done in one of the 3 ways – linear probing where the next interval to be probed is fixed at 1, quadratic probing where the distance between the probes is determined by a quadratic equation, or double hashing where the probing interval is fixed by another hashing function even though it is fixed for each record. While linear probing offers the best caching it fails miserably at clustering. Double hashing has no clustering issues but its cache performance is pathetic. Quadratic probing is considerably the better option since it balances caching and clustering better than the other two options.

64: What are the differences between Chaining and Open Addressing?

Answer:

Chaining is the simplest way for collision resolution in hash tables. Though it uses more space because of the pointers, chaining can be done using the simplest of data structures. Chaining usually does not involve any clustering issues whereas clustering is a major issue with open addressing. Chaining is a better method to adopt performance-wise.

Chaining makes the degradation a little more refined. The larger the records, chaining uses lesser space to store them. In open addressing, storing smaller records is more efficient but storing larger records is expensive in terms of the memory used. Open addressing makes the hash table easy to serialize since no address is stored.

65: What are the problems with hash tables?

Answer:

Even though hash tables are considered good for implementing caching, hash tables take a lot of time performing the hash functions. Since the data stored in the slots are distributed randomly in the memory, it takes up more time in allocation and seeking information. First the index has to be searched for the next address and then the data in the address is accessed. Hash functions are quite complex and prone to errors. Since there are many hash functions used along with each hash table, it can be quite difficult to manage the hash functions. Moreover, a poorly written hash function can result in unwarranted collisions which affect the program performance adversely.

66: Explain Probabilistic hashing.

Answer:

Probabilistic hashing is the easiest way to implement hashing in the memory. In fact, caching is implemented using this technique. When collision occurs, the old record in the same slot is either replaced by the new records or the records to be inserted is dropped. Even though it may end up in losing the earlier data, the method is comparatively easier to implement and performs well when the earlier records are not required. A bit array or bloom filter implements the same functionality.

67: Explain Perfect hashing.

Answer:

Perfect hashing is when the slots for each record are uniquely mapped. This happens only when the number of items to be stored and the items are constant. Perfect hashing cannot be guaranteed but by constructing a very large hash table, we can expect the slots to be mapped uniquely without any issue. This is easier to implement, lessens the probability of collisions and dispenses the data evenly across the hash table. This may affect the memory usage and performance since even for a smaller amount data, the entire hash table may have to be searched. If we have quite a lot of data with empty slots in between also, the search and insert may take longer time.

68: Explain Coalesced hashing.

Answer:

Coalesced hashing uses a combination of open address and chaining methods. It creates a chain of items stored in the table and when collision occurs, instead of storing in another table, it stores the colliding data in the same table as a chain. There's no clustering issue as with open address, but similar to the open addressing pattern, the next available space in the same table is used up. The first available slot in the hash table is used as a collision bucket. Whenever a collision occurs, the new record is pushed into the bucket and the address is linked to the colliding slot. It works similar to chaining but is not as complicated to implement. Like chaining, it links the address of the colliding record but like open address, it stores the information in the next bucket slot available.

69: Explain Extendible hashing.

Answer:

In extendible hashing, the table bucket only is extended or resized as required which makes it respond faster to time-sensitive programs. Every time a resize is required, the bucket is either recreated or a new bucket is created by adding a bit to the existing index to include the additional members and a mapping to the earlier bit array is updated or created. If the existing bit array was 00, 01, 10, 11, if you want to add a 5th element, the bit mask is appended by another bit to the front like 000, 001, 010, and 011. Then further 100, 101, 110, and 111 becomes the new entries in the new table. 00 will point to 000 and 001, 01 to 010, 10 to 011 and similarly each element of the 2 bit array will point to the corresponding one in the 3 bit array.

70: Explain Linear hashing.

Answer:

In linear hashing, every time an overflow occurs, the hash table is resized and the new items are rehashed with the incremented hash table size. When the overflow occurs initially, it adds on to the bucket first and only when the bucket overflows, the hash table is resized and the entire table is rehashed. Every time the bucket overflows, the new values are rehashed and then allotted in the new slot created one at a time. The main point to note here is that buckets can be split whether it is half of fully occupied.

This page is intentionally left blank.

Chapter 7

Trees

71: Explain the Tree data structure.

Answer:

A tree has a root element with 1 or 2 nodes attached to each node. It is a hierarchical data structure used to store information in an ordered way. A binary tree can have zero to maximum 2 child nodes. The uppermost element or node is called the root and the lowermost element or node that has no child node is called a leaf node. The number of elements that connects a particular node from the root to that node determines the depth of a node. The height of a node is determined by the length of the node to its deepest leaf. A tree's height is determined by the height of its root.

72: What are the properties of a tree?

Answer:

Every tree has at least one child node in the hierarchical structure. There's a root element in all trees which form the center of the tree. Every node has a child element or else, it is called a leaf. Every child node or leaf has a parent node. The root has no parent and it is the parent of other nodes of the tree. A binary tree typically has 0, 1 or 2 child nodes.

73: Explain Node, Edge, Leaf, and Root of a tree.

Answer:

Each and every element of a tree, except the root is called a node of the tree. Each node can have a maximum of 2 child nodes. For a tree with x number of nodes, there'll be x-1 nodes in the tree. Edge is the link that connects any two nodes. Leaf is the bottom most node of a tree. It will not have any child node. Root is the topmost node of a tree. It marks the beginning of the tree. A tree can have only one root but each sub-tree will have its own root.

74: Differentiate among Parent, Sibling and Subtree of a tree.

Answer:

A node is the parent node of the nodes linked below it. Siblings are nodes in the same level of the same parent. A subtree is a tree within a main tree which has multiple child nodes that has their own child nodes. For example,

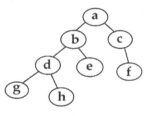

Here, a is the root. Its child nodes are b and c and they are
siblings. B is the parent node for d and e. A subtree is formed
by b, d, e, g, and h nodes. D and e are siblings just as g and h
are.

75: What is a red-black tree?
Answer:

A red-black tree is a self-balancing binary search tree. Even
though the tree balancing is not perfect, the nodes contain an
additional bit for marking it black or red based on certain
property checks. The ordering and colour coding is redone
upon every change in the tree via insert, update or delete. The
colouring makes it easy to arrange it easily every time the tree
data is changed. Since the colour code is only one bit, it does
not consume much memory too. In a red-black tree, the root is
always black. The nodes can be red or black based on its
properties. A red node's child nodes are always black. The leaf
nodes are always black.

76: Explain Tree Traversal.
Answer:

Tree traversal means visiting the tree nodes in a particular order. There are 3 patterns to traverse a tree – preorder, postorder and inorder. Each method adopts a different pattern and the programmer can also implement one of these patterns based on the actual requirement. Traversal is required to search for a particular node or data. Traversal is also required to perform an insert or delete when the node position is not known. Even though most of the traversals start from the root, it can start from any node and travel either ways of the node.

77: Explain Preorder.

Answer:

The preorder traversal starts from the root. The left subtrees are traversed first and then the right subtrees are traversed. In the below tree, the traversal begins at 'a'. The subtree with 'b' as the root is traversed first and them the subtree with 'c' as the root is considered. The order in which this tree is traversed is a->b->d->g->h->e->c->f.

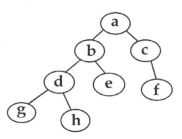

78: Explain Postorder.

Answer:

In postorder traversal method, the root is the last node visited. First the left subtrees are visited and then the right subtrees and finally only the root is visited. In the below tree structure, the first visited node will be 'g' and the last visited one will be 'a' which is the root. The order of traversal is g->h->d->e->b->f->c->a.

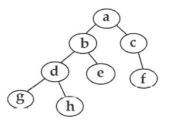

79: Explain Inorder.

Answer:

Inorder traversal begins at the left subtree, then it reaches the root and then moves to the right subtree. In the below tree structure, 'g' is the first visited node and 'c' is the last visited one. The traversal is done in the order g->d->h->b->e->a->f->c.

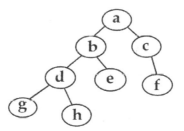

80: Explain a binary search tree.

Answer:

A binary search tree is a binary tree with all nodes lesser than the root to the left of it and all the nodes greater than the root to its right. In a binary search tree, all child nodes will also follow this pattern. Every parent will have nodes lesser than itself to its left and greater than the parent to its right. A binary search tree or BST is also called an ordered tree because of this. This type of data structure is best when we need to store data in an ordered manner like a dictionary or directory which is ordered alphabetically.

81: Explain a Trie.

Answer:

A Trie is a special type of tree data structure where the node is not represented by a key. It is instead identified by its position and the parent in the tree. A trie data structure is only used for special purposes where the key is not as important as its position. A Trie is also known as a Prefix tree or a radix tree. It is like an ordered array which is usually used to store strings. A dictionary implementation is a perfect example of the trie. The following image will give you an idea why a trie is also called a Prefix tree.

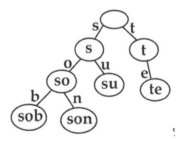

82: Explain BSF and DSF for BST.

Answer:

BSF is Breadth First Traversal and DSF is Depth First Traversal.

The popular patterns used for tree traversal are DSF such as Inorder, preorder and postorder. BSF pattern is also known as the level order pattern and it considers the nodes at each level in the order and then moves to the next level which is way different from the DSF patterns. In the below given tree,

Inorder traversal is done in the order g->d->h->b->e->a->f->c

Preorder traversal is done in the order a->b->d->g->h->e->c->f

PostInorder traversal is done in the order g->h->d->e->b->f->c->a

BSF is done in the order a->b->c->d->e->f->g->h

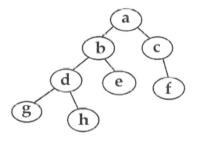

83: What are the differences between BSF and DSF for BST?

Answer:

BSF is breadth first traversal and DSF is depth first traversal, both use different methods for traversing the tree. While BSF considers each level at a time, DSF essentially considers each subtree at a time. Even though there's not much difference in the time required for these 4 types of traversals, the difference comes in the extra space required for each type of traversal. Since DSF considers the height of the tree, the maximum extra space required for DSF is $O(x)$ where x is the maximum height of the tree. Since BSF considers the width at each level of the tree, the maximum extra space required for BSF is O(y) where y is the maximum width of tree. Moreover, DSF is recursive in nature and hence involves additional recursive function overheads. Where the nodes are the base for search, DSF is a better option and where the root is the base for traversal, BSF is a better option.

84: Explain a Spanning Tree.

Answer:

A spanning tree is related to a network graph where every node appears at least once in the tree. Even though the minimum spanning tree or MST does not assure the shortest distance between 2 nodes, it assures that the total weight of the tree remains minimal. It is organized such that the total weight between the nodes remains minimal throughout the tree. A spanning tree, especially the MST can be used to implement the best network graph for a computer network, telecommunications, transportation and electrical grids.

85: How do you convert a binary tree into a doubly linked list?

Answer:

To convert a binary tree into a doubly linked list, the main job is to make all the left pointers to previous and right pointers to next. The first element of the linked list has to be the left most leaf of the tree. The tree is traversed inorder and each element is picked and posted to the doubly linked list.

The following tree will be stored in the doubly linked list as

Tree

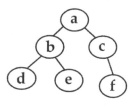

Doubly Linked List

Head   Tail

D			B		E		A		F		C	
Nu ll	Nex t B	Pre v D	Nex t E	Prev B	Next A	Prev E	Next F	Prev A	Next C	Prev F	Nu ll

86: How do you convert a doubly linked list into a balanced BST?

Answer:

Suppose I have a doubly linked list sorted in the ascending order 10, 12, 14, 16, 18, 20, 22 to convert it into a binary tree, I need to find the middle most element and make it the root. Take the left half and right half and repeat the process to create subtrees on either side. So the above linked list will be converted into a balanced BST like this

Linked list 10, 12, 14, 16, 18, 20, 22

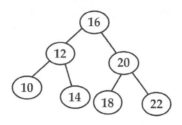

87: What is a Threaded Binary Tree?

Answer:

A threaded binary tree makes inorder traversal easier in a BST. A BST is made binary by making its usually null right node pointers to point to its successor in the inorder traversal mode. This way in the below given tree, 10's right node will point to 12, 14th right node to 16, and 18's right node to 20. This avoids recursion and makes the inorder traversal faster. Threaded binary can be done in 2 ways. The singly threaded model is as explained above. In doubly threaded model, the right node points to the successor as above and the left node to the predecessor node. This facilitates reverse inorder and postorder traversals.

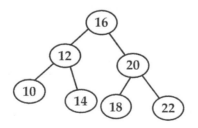

88: What is an AVL Tree?

Answer:

AVL trees are also called balanced binary search trees. It was invented by Georgy Adelson Velsky and Evgenii Landis, and hence the name AVL. The AVL trees maintain the balance factor as 1, meaning the difference between the heights of the right subtrees and left subtrees will be 1 in an AVL tree. This balance factor is maintained by rebalancing the tree every time the data or elements are changed with an insert, update, or delete. It is essentially like a red-black tree but quite faster since the AVL tree is more rigidly balanced than a red-black tree.

89: How do you find the height of a node in a tree?

Answer:

The height of a node in a tree is the length of the longest path from it to its outermost leaf. To find the height x of a node in the tree t, a recursive function height is used which finds the distance from x to its last leaf in the subtree and 1 is added to it. So it is height (x) = 1 + height(x, t). If x is a leaf, then its height is 0. Otherwise, for each node in tree t that comes after x, a counter is incremented which counts the height till x becomes the leaf.

90: How do you insert into an ordered BST?

Answer:

The very first step for inserting into an ordered BST is to find out whether the element to be inserted is greater than or less than the root. If it is greater than the root, we can concentrate only on the right side of the tree and otherwise only on the left of the root. The insert is also recursive like most of the tree functions. The subtrees are all checked for the key against the key to be inserted. The correct position is found out when it encounters a leaf or a node with no left child when the key is less than the node or the node with no right child when the key is greater than the node.

91: How do you delete from an ordered BST?

Answer:

Deleting from an ordered BST can get tricky in some cases. There are three scenarios to consider:

a) First, if the node to be deleted is a leaf node, then the delete is simple; we just need to delete the node.

b) Second, if the node to be deleted has a single child, the child has to move up the tree to where the deleted node was and link the parent to the child of the deleted node.

c) Third is the most difficult scenario to handle, when we have to delete a node which has 2 child nodes. In this case, we can either choose the lowest element from the right subtree or find the largest element in the left subtree of the node to be deleted. Replace the node to be deleted by this node and delete the minimum value node or maximum value node from where it was earlier using the earlier 2 conditions.

92: How do you search in an ordered BST?

Answer:

Searching is an ordered BST is very easy. Since it is ordered, you can use a recursive function and check whether the key to be searched is the root of the BST. If the key is not the root, more to the right of the tree and search the subtrees if the key is greater than root or else, do the same to the left subtree of the root. Use a recursive function and pass the parent node till you reach the leaf. Keep a flat ready when you get the searched key and exit the recursion as soon as you find the key. Or else, the flag will be set to false and the key is not found in the tree.

93: How do you find out whether a tree is full Binary or not?

Answer:

A full binary tree is one with either zero child nodes or 2 child nodes. So to check whether a given binary tree is full binary or not, we have to use a recursive function to check the following conditions:

a) First, if the node has no nodes, it is full binary

b) Second, if the node has both left and right nodes (not null nodes), it is full binary

c) Third, use a recursive function to check the first and second conditions for each subtree till you reach the leaf. Keep a flag open and set it to false, whenever one of the 2 conditions go false and exit the recursion.

94: How do you create a binary tree from an array?

Answer:

When you have a sorted array, to convert it into a BST, find the middle-most element and make it the root. Then add the values larger than the root to the right of the root making subtrees as you have more elements. Similarly, add values smaller than the root to the left of the root making subtrees as you have more elements this side. The issue comes when you have an unsorted array or an array which is being input by the user. In such a case, if the unsorted array has the values 10, 9, 12, 5, 8 then the binary tree is created by making 10 as the root and then arrange the rest of elements to its left or right as it is smaller or larger than 10. So the tree would be -

Tree

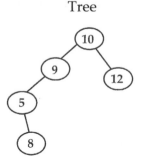

95: What is an expression tree?

Answer:

An expression tree is one with leaves as the operands and the internal nodes as the operators. If you traverse the tree using the inorder pattern, it gives the infix version of the postfix expression. Similarly, if you traverse using the preorder pattern, it comes up with a prefix expression. Postfix expressions are evaluated using postorder traversal pattern. For example, the expression (a-b)*(c+d) is represented in the following way using an expression tree:

Expression Tree

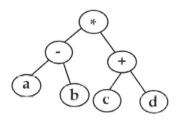

96: How do you evaluate an expression tree?

Answer:

The easiest way to evaluate an expression tree is using the inorder traversal pattern. If you have an expression tree as below,

Expression Tree

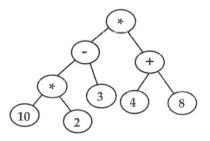

In the inorder traversal mode, this expression can be evaluated as ((10*2)-3)*(4+8) which is equal to 17 * 12 = 204. Here each subtree is put as an expression unit put within a bracket. So it becomes easier to evaluate without any confusion.

97: What is a symmetric tree?

Answer:

A Symmetric tree is a tree with both sides as a mirror image. That is, one side of the tree is a mirror image of the other side. The following is an example of a symmetric tree:

Expression Tree

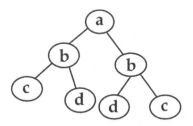

A tree is said to be symmetric if the left nodes of a parent corresponds to the right nodes of the parent and vice versa. As with any tree, a recursive function isMirror() can be used to check if each subtree is symmetric or not.

98: How do you find the largest number in a binary tree?

Answer:

In a BST, to find the largest number is easy. We can traverse the right subtree and find out the largest key from it. Similarly, if you want to find the smallest key from the BST, just traverse the left subtree of the root till you find the smallest node. But when it comes to an unordered binary tree, the best way to find the smallest or the largest key is to use a recursive function to find the max or min among the parent, right node and left node of each subtree in each level and use it to compare with the next level.

99: How do you find the level of a node in tree?

Answer:

The level of a node is its distance from the root. To find the level of a given key, you have to use a recursive function and a counter that's incremented inside it with every call till the key is found. This counter is set to 0 initially and if the key is not found, it remains 0 indicating that the key was never found in the tree. Otherwise, check the key, if it is greater than the root, check the right side subtrees recursively or else, check the left side subtrees recursively till you find the key or reach the leaf.

100: What is a Ternary search tree?

Answer:

A Ternary tree is a special tree where each node contains 3 pointers, one which points to the left node, one to the right node and another to a node with value equal to the current node. The left pointer points to a node which is smaller than the current node and the right pointer points to a node larger than the current node. Each node also has 2 more sections, one is the data to be stored and the other denotes the end of string or a bit value that indicates whether it is a leaf node or not. Ternary search trees are more space efficient.

This page is intentionally left blank.

Chapter 8

Sets

101: What is a set?

Answer:

A set is a collection of unique elements, related to each other in some way and need not be in any order. You can consider a set of all football players of a team where none of the names are repeated and the names need not be stored in any order. But they are all related as players of the same team. We cannot add any other member or element in this set. A set of students who belong to a class is also another implementation. We cannot add another class' student in one class' set.

102: What are the generally used implementations of sets?

Answer:

The Set data structure is generally implemented as a List, Bit

Array, or an Associative Array that contains unique elements that are related to each other in some way. A Linear list is the simplest implementation of a set data structure. A Bit Array will contain 1 or 0 (Boolean *true* or *false*) as the element and it is generally used as a flag property of complex data structures. Associative Arrays are the hash tables and binary search trees that contain unique elements that are related to each other. It is a more complex implementation where the information contained is usually ordered.

103: What is a Null Set? What is its use?

Answer:

A Null Set contains no element. It is used in cases where the set is populated dynamically by an expression which may result in no elements. It is useful when we are not sure whether or not the set will be populated during the runtime. Null or Empty sets can be used with database tables when we are not sure whether the table exists or whether it has any records or not. Empty Sets are useful when the set is dynamically populated.

104: What are the basic operations you can do with a set?

Answer:

All sets allow 3 basic operations - Union, Intersection, Difference, and Subset. A Union returns the combination of elements of 2 or more sets without violating the set rules. The 2 set rules to be considered are that the elements are unique and related. An Intersection returns all the common elements of 2 sets. A Difference operation returns all the elements of the first set that are not in the second set. A subset operation returns 1 when the first set contains elements that are a subset of the second set. Otherwise it returns 0.

| Union | Intersection | Difference | Subset |

105: What are the different types of Sets?

Answer:

Sets can be categorized as Mutable and Immutable sets. Mutable sets are dynamic in nature which means it can be created during the runtime as and when required. The size of the mutable set can be fixed during the runtime. Similarly, you can dynamically add elements into and delete elements from a mutable set. The possible operations on a mutable set are create, add, delete and capacity. An Immutable set is static in nature. It can only contain pre-determined number of values. Even though you can create the set during the runtime, once created, it remains static. You cannot add or delete from an Immutable set. The possible operations on an Immutable set are elementOf, empty, size and build. Elementof returns whether the given value is an element of the set or not. Empty returns whether it is an empty set or now. Size returns the size or the number of elements in the set. Build lets you create the set and insert the elements into the set. Build returns the address of the first element of the set.

106: Explain the Bit Vector representation of sets.

Answer:

Sometimes the information required to be stored is only like a flag value or bit values 0 or 1, like the Boolean *true* or *false*. In such cases, a BitArray or Bit Vector representation is used which requires very little storage compared to any other data type. If the requirement is for a set that contains information on whether the particular student is above 18 years or not, a bit array representation will be the better choice. A bit array with values {0, 0, 1, 0, 1, 0, 0} means that out of 7 students, the 1st record corresponds to a student who is not yet 18 years old. The second student is also aged less than 18 years. The 3rd and 5th students are 18 or above and the rest of them are less than 18 years old.

107: What are disjoint sets?

Answer:

A disjoint set is a set that contains many subsets, usually singleton sets that never overlaps with each other. Each subset can be considered as a linked list with the first element as the head. You can add more elements to it by pointing to the other subsets. Disjoint sets allow 3 basic operations – find, union and makeset. Find lets you search for a particular subset or element. Union lets you join multiple subsets within the set. MakeSet lets you create a subset which is like adding a new element. Disjoint sets are used to implement undirected graphs, to check whether 2 or more vertices belong to the same graph object.

108: What is a Sparse Set?

Answer:

A Sparse set is like a bit vector but the elements are not bits but indices of another large array. When we have a very large array of values to handle, all sort, search, insert, delete and update operations become very difficult to manage. In the Sparse Set concept, the entire array is split into dense and sparse where the dense array contains the elements and the sparse array contains the indices which makes searching in the dense array quite simple. You can also perform unions and intersection using a sparse set

This page is intentionally left blank.

Chapter 9

Graphs

109: What is a Graph data structure?

Answer:

A Graph data structure contains a set of arrays called vertices and a set of edges. Every edge will have 2 vertices that point to a location of the edge. Graphs are used to implement images or networks wherein the edges or elements are related to each other in some way or the other. Every graph will have edges, vertices, path and adjacency. A graph can be represented as a tree data structure. The Vertex is the node. The Edge determines the path or the order in which other nodes are linked in the tree. Adjacency determines the nodes directly linked to another node by a path. A Path is the series of edges to traverse to reach a particular node.

110: What is the difference between Graph and a Tree data structure?

Answer:

Even though a Graph can be represented by a tree, it is a special kind of tree. In a typical Tree data structure, two nodes are connected by a single path, but in a Graph data structure, a node can be connected to another node in many ways. For the same reason, a Tree cannot form a loop of nodes while a Graph may form a loop. Every Tree data structure has a root which forms the base of the tree. A Graph does not have a root concept. For the same reason, a Tree has a parent – child relation while the Graph has no such relation. A Tree implements a hierarchical model while a Graph implements a network model.

111: Explain Vertex, Edge, Adjacency and Path in a Graph.

Answer:

The Vertex is can be considered as the node or element of the Graph. If you consider the following Graph representation, A, B, C, D, E and F are the vertices. Edge connects 2 vertices and it is the path to be taken for traversing through the Graph. 0, 1, 2, 3, 4, and 5 represent the path. Adjacency is the connection between 2 nodes. A node is said to be adjacent to another node if they are connected directly by an edge. A is adjacent to B but B is not adjacent to C while A and D are adjacent to C since they have an edge connecting them to C. A Path is the order in which a node connects to another node. For A to connect to E, it has to take the path ABE. A can connect to D by AD or ACD. B can connect to C by BAC.

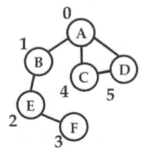

112: What are the different types of Graphs?

Answer:

Graphs can be classified as Directed, Undirected or Weighted Graphs. In a Directed Graph, the edges points from one vertex to another, indicating the direction of traversing. A Directed graph's in-degree means the number of edges that point towards a node. A Directed graph's out-degree means the number of edges that point from a node. In an Undirected graph, the nodes are connected by edges but the direction of the path is not given which means if there's a path, it can be used for traversal either way. Weighted graphs will represent the cost of the path or some value associated with the path. When the path contains the distance between 2 vertices, it becomes a weighted graph.

113: Explain Graph representations.

Answer:

The commonly used Graph Representations are Adjacency List

and Adjacency Matrix. Adjacency Matrix can be looked upon as a two-dimensional array based on the number of vertices in the Graph. There will be x * x elements in the array if x is the number of vertices in the Graph. Adjacency list can be looked upon as a linked list with the number of vertices as in the Graph. Each array element corresponds to a linked list based on the adjacency of that vertex. While the Adjacency matrix is easier to implement, it consumes more storage space. The Adjacency list is a little complex to understand but requires less space to implement.

114: What are the basic operations in a Graph?

Answer:

Every Graph allows 3 basic operations – Add Vertex, Add Edge and Display Vertex. Add Vertex operation lets you add a node or Vertex to the graph. Add Edge lets you add the edge or path between two vertices. Display Vertex lets you display a particular vertex of the graph. Other than these, you can do Depth First and Breadth First traversals in a Graph. You can also check whether a particular Vertex is reachable from another vertex with the IsReachable operator.

115: Explain the IsReachable function implementation.

Answer:

The IsReachable function specifies whether a particular node or vertex is reachable from another node or vertex. It basically lets you know whether or not these 2 vertices are connected by a series of edges in any way. This is particularly important when dealing with directed graphs where even if there is a path from x to y vertex, if it is directed only one side, then there's no path from y to x, if that's the only path between these two vertices. The following figure will explain the same. Here, IsReachable(graph, A, C) will return true but IsReachable(graph, C, A) will return false.

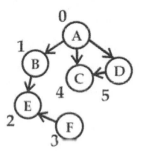

116: Explain Graph traversals.

Answer:

Graph traversals can be done Breadth First or Depth First. In Breadth First traversal, the graph is traversed breadth-wise first. It means that from the Vertex we are searching, it checks the vertices that are adjacent to it first and then move to the next available vertex and continue the same pattern. Once a vertex's all adjacent paths are covered, it is marked as visited, printed and removed from the queue. This continues till all the vertices are removed from the queue. In Depth First traversal, each path is traversed depth-wise till there's no vertex left in the path. If the Graph is Undirected, the best possible path is continued till we reach the last vertex in the path. All visited vertices are marked, displayed and pushed into a stack. When you reach one end, pop the vertex until you find one which has other adjacent vertices and continue the process till the stack goes empty.

117: Explain DFS in Graph.

Answer:

In Depth First Search, for each vertex, the prioritised path is considered first and the adjacent vertex is taken. If the vertex has other edges connected to it, its prioritised path is considered and the adjacent vertex is taken. Each visited vertex is flagged as visited and is displayed. That vertex is then pushed into a stack. Once you reach the end of one path, the last visited vertex is popped out and the next path is considered and the process continues till the stack becomes empty. In the figure given below, the path taken is ABEF first, then ACDA. In 2 steps the traversal completes.

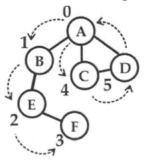

118: Explain BFS in Graph.

Answer:

In Breath First Search, the adjacent vertices are searched first.

Once all the adjacent vertices of a vertex are searched, it takes up the next level of vertices. Every visited vertex is marked as visited and displayed. Every visited vertex is inserted into a queue and as soon as there's no more adjacent vertex, it is removed from the queue. The process continues till the queue becomes empty. The following figure will explain Breadth First Search better. Here, AB, AC and AD are traversed first. Then BE is considered and at last EF is checked. Here we need 3 levels.

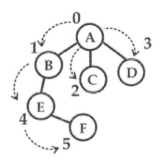

119: Explain some of the common applications of Graph

Answer:

Graphs are commonly used to represent Maps, networks, GPS etc. Whenever we have to plot values over an area and only the position is known, it is represented as a Graph. Moreover, Graphs help us extensively to draw the relation between the elements and to find the best possible route for traversal or to reach from one node to another. It also shows in how many ways and which all ways each node is connected to another node. Railway, Telephone and Computer networks can be easily represented in a Graph. Similarly, locations and GPS require a Graph representation. Pipelines, real estate and travel routes are also well-represented by Graphs.

120: How do you represent a graph using a matrix?

Answer:

Adjacency matrix can be used to represent a graph. The matrix's size will be x * x where x is the number of vertices in the Graph. If the Graph has 4 Vertices, a matrix of size 16 will be required to represent the graph.

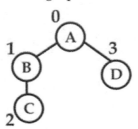

To represent this graph, the following matrix can be used.

mat	0	1	2	3
0	0	1	0	1
1	1	0	1	0
2	0	1	0	0
3	1	0	0	0

mat[0][1] = 1 means there is an edge between 0th and 1st vertex (A-B) in the graph.

mat[2][0] = 0 means there is no edge between 2nd and 0th (C-A) vertex in the graph.

121: Explain Adjacency Matrix.

Answer:

Adjacency matrix is used to represent the adjacent matrices in a Graph. When we have a Graph with 5 vertices, it can be represented by a matrix of size 5 * 5 or 25 columns.

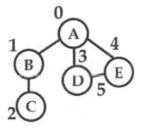

To represent this graph, the following matrix can be used.

Mat	A	B	C	D	E
A	0	1	0	1	1
B	1	0	1	0	0
C	0	1	0	0	0
D	1	0	0	0	1
E	1	0	0	1	0

mat[A][B] = 1 means there is an adjacency between the vertices A and B in the graph.

mat[C][A] = 0 means there is no adjacency between C and A vertices in the graph.

mat[E][A] = 1 means there is an adjacency between E and A vertices in the graph.

mat[E][D] = 1 means there is an adjacency between E and D vertices in the graph.

mat[D][E] = 1 means there is an adjacency between D and E vertices in the graph (because this is an undirected graph).

122: What are the advantages and disadvantages of Adjacency Matrix?

Answer:

Adjacency matrices are easier to implement and manage. They are easier to code. The adjacency matrix makes adding and deleting edges easier to implement. The major issues with adjacency matrix are:

a) When we have to deal with large graphs, the matrix consumes a lot of memory. If the graph has x vertices, the matrix has to be of x * x size. Even though it can be dealt by using Sparse sets, the same implementation becomes too expensive for a sparse graph while it is worth for dense graphs.

b) Another issue is that adding and deleting vertices can get quite complex with adjacency matrices. They perform well for analysis purposes.

c) The last and an important issue with adjacent matrix is that when you want to know the adjacent edges of the current vertex and you are implementing DFS algorithm, it becomes very complex.

123: Explain Adjacency List.

Answer:

Adjacency lists are used to represent a graph as a linked list. To represent the following graph in an adjacency list, for each node or vertex of the graph a corresponding linked list is formed with its adjacent vertices.

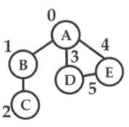

The Adjacency list for the above graph is

A -> B, D, E

B -> Λ, C

C -> B

D -> A, E

E -> A, D

124: What are the advantages and disadvantages of Adjacency List?

Answer:

The Adjacency list is a compact form of representing a Graph. Sparse graphs are best represented with adjacency lists, as the Adjacency list requires less memory. Using an Adjacency list is the easier way to find the shortest path between 2 vertices. Considering these advantages, Adjacency lists also have some disadvantages as below:

a) Managing edges using an adjacency list is very complex, particularly with dense graphs.

b) Dynamically deleting a vertex also becomes very complex since the adjacencies have to be rearranged. But adding the vertex is not as complex.

c) Dense graphs represented in adjacency list require more memory than an adjacency matrix

d) Adjacency checking takes more time using Adjacency lists, particularly when they are not sorted.

125: What do you mean by cost of a graph?

Answer:

Cost of a graph determines the cost involved in terms of the distance travelled or time taken to traverse through the graph Depth First or Breadth First. When a vertex is connected to another through an edge, the path will carry a cost for traversal which can be measured in terms of speed, distance, time or any other 'weight' as relevant to the graph representation. For example, when you have a network of computers, the time for response might be the weight or the amount of information transferred can be another weightage. But in the case of a location map, the distance covered or the time taken to reach might be the weightage. The cost of a graph is basically that total weightage to traverse through the graph by DSF or BSF.

126: Explain the Minimum Spanning Tree problem.

Answer:

A minimum Spanning Tree Problem is to find out the shortest path between two vertices or the least costing path between two vertices, given that there are n edges connecting those 2 vertices. This is a typical problem that arises frequently in the real-time scenario. Suppose you need to establish an internal phone network (like an extension or an intercom network) within an apartment complex that connects every apartment with every other apartment in the complex. The network operator will have to work out the least-cost plan that will connect every apartment with every other apartment. Or to make it simple consider establishing extensions within a house. The house has 6 rooms and every room needs to be connected to each other. The idea is to find the least-cost path from one node to another and connect them.

127: How are Graphs advantageous in implementing real-time solutions?

Answer:

Graphs are the best way to represent a group of location-specific nodes that are related to each other. Networks and roadmaps are better represented through graphs as they clearly show how every location is connected to another location and how much does it cost to reach the other location, in terms or distance, time or fuel consumption, whichever is relevant to the user. Graphs can be implemented in different ways depending on its requirements. Graphs are the best way to represent all types of networks and scenarios with multiple dependency or relation.

128: What is Incidence matrix?

Answer:

An Incidence Matrix represents a graph in a specific way. Incidence Matrix will have vertices * edges number of elements. The vertices are represented by rows and the edges to each vertex are represented by columns. The matrix has 0s, 1s and 2s. Each neighbour is represented by a 1 in the column and if the same column has a 2 against another vertex, it is a neighbour too. All 1s represent edges from a vertex and all 2s represent edges to the vertex.

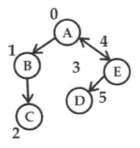

This graph is represented as:

A	1	0	0	2
B	2	1	0	0
C	0	2	0	0
D	0	0	0	2
E	2	0	0	1

129: What is Incidence list?

Answer:

The incidence list stores the linked list of edges that starts from a particular vertex. So for each vertex, it will have as many elements in the linked list as it has adjacencies starting from that vertex.

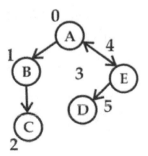

This graph is represented as:

A – {<A, B>, <A, E>}

B – {<B, C>}

C – {}

D – {}

E – {<E, A>, <E, D>}

This is much simpler to manage since when you add a vertex, you can just add a new linked list with the new vertex and add the edges to its linked list. Finding the edges becomes a little complex as you have to go through each vertex's linked list and find the edges list.

130: How do you find the shortest path in a Graph?

Answer:

The shortest path from one vertex to another can be calculated using the Breadth First Search method. At any given point, in

BSF, the weightage of each level of traversal from a vertex is available since it considers all the adjacent vertices first and then goes to the next level of adjacency. By weightage, we mean the distance of one vertex to its adjacent vertex. In the following figure, the weightage of traversing from A to B is 5, from B to E is 2, From E to F is 1 so from A to F the total weightage is 8.

The weightage of traversing from A to C is 1, from C to F is 3 so from A to F can be 4.

So here the shortest path from A to F is through C which weighs only 4 points. This is determined when the 5th step is completed since by then 1 path to F is already found which weighs 4 points and the next parallel path already weighs 7 points.

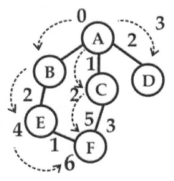

Algorithms

This page is intentionally left blank.

Chapter 10

General Concepts Of Algorithms

131: What do you mean by Algorithm?

Answer:

Algorithm is basically the step by step procedure involved in solving a computer problem. Once you have the login in place, clearly specified with the loops and ifs, you can easily implement it in any programming language. It is based on this algorithm that a more refined Flowchart is prepared which is used by the programmers to write it in a particular programming language. You can develop algorithms for the simplest processes to very complex procedures such as database programming. To understand an algorithm, it can be followed step by step simulating with possible values of input.

132: What are input specialized and strategy specialized algorithms?

Answer:

Algorithms can be broadly classified as input specialized and strategy specialized. Input specialized algorithms are used when the finiteness of the data being input can be determined during the implementation of the process. If we know how many elements will be input during the runtime, an input specialized algorithm is used. Set Algorithm, Sequence Algorithm, Matrix Algorithm etc. are some commonly used input algorithms. Strategy specialized algorithms are used when the finiteness is not known. Recursion, dynamic programming etc. are strategy specialized algorithms.

133: What are the different types of input specialized Algorithms commonly used?

Answer:

Input specialized algorithms are used when the size of the input is finite. For example, when a predefined list or array of information has to be processed or some repeated processing has to be done for a finite number of times, one of the algorithms are used Set Algorithm, Polynomial Algorithm, Sequence Algorithm, Graph Algorithm or Matrix Algorithm. For these algorithms, the number of items or iterations is finite and hence can be directly dealt with (without using any recursion or pointer arithmetic). These are rather simple to implement even though the programs may stretch longer because of the data structures in use.

134: What are the different Strategy specialized algorithms?
Answer:

When we cannot determine the finiteness of a process or iteration, we will have to use one of the commonly used strategy specialized algorithms such as Divide-and-Conquer Algorithm, Greedy Algorithm, Dynamic Programming Algorithm, or Iterative Algorithm. Here, sometimes, the entire process is divided into biteable chunks of smaller named processes that can be repeatedly called in a loop or recursively. Some others use iteration and conditional termination of the process. Dynamic programming involves using pointers extensively to allocate memory to build arrays and other collections.

135: Explain Divide-and-Conquer Algorithm.
Answer:

In the Divide and Conquer algorithm, the entire problem is divided into smaller, reusable processes or procedures. These procedures or smaller chunks of processes are repeatedly used to solve the problem. Finally, the processes and iterations are combined appropriately to arrive at the desired solution. Recursion and iterative function calling are the usual methods adopted in this algorithm. The search and sort algorithms are best examples of implementations of divide and conquer algorithms.

136: Give some examples of Divide-and-Conquer Algorithm.

Answer:

Some of the commonly used implementations of Divide and Conquer algorithm are:

a) **Binary Search** – Used to search for an element in a sorted array. Starts from the middle of the array and works its way to the right if the value to be searched is greater than the middle element and to the left if the value to be searched is less than the middle element. For each section, the above-mentioned process continues either till the element is found or till there's no element to be searched.

b) **Merge Sort** – Divides the entire array till it gets down to each element. For each pass, each element is checked against the next element and swapped if element1 > element2. The next 2 elements are considered and the process is repeated. The entire process is repeated till there's no swapping happening.

c) **Quick Sort** – Takes the last element as the pivot value and splits the entire array into values holding less than pivot and larger than pivot. The pivot is pushed into the middle. Each partition continues the process till it is fully sorted.

137: Explain Dynamic Programming Algorithm.

Answer:

Dynamic programming algorithms are similar to divide and

rule algorithms in the sense that they break down the problem into smaller, reusable units. But they also make use of the previously resolved answer and use it to derive at the next solution. The Fibonacci series and Tower of Hanoi problems given below are perfect examples of dynamic programming algorithm. For finding the Fibonacci series, the previous answer is stored in a variable and reused for each recursive function call.

138: Give some examples of Dynamic Programming Algorithm.

Answer:

Some of the commonly used Dynamic Programming Algorithm are:

a) **Fibonacci Series** – Here each number is arrived at by adding the previous two numbers. The process of finding the next number is the same so it is reused by recursion or iteration. At every stage, the previous 2 numbers are stored such that they are available to arrive at the next number.

b) **Knapsack Problem** – Here a knapsack is given which can hold a maximum capacity of weight and different smaller weights of different items are given. The idea is to fill the knapsack optimally such that maximum items are included in the knapsack while keeping it within the specified weight. It is done by considering subsets of items that are either taken or not taken into the knapsack. No item is taken partially. Each subset's weight is calculated and from the available weighted subsets, the one with maximum weight which is less than the allowed weight is considered.

c) **Weighted Project Scheduling** – This is finding out the profitability of each project from a set of projects with each having the start and end times and its profit associated. The trick here is to get the jobs with maximum profit without overlapping the time. Given the set of projects, each project's time and profitability are considered and compared with the next one for time overlapping. The overlapping ones and the less profitable ones are dropped instantly.

139: Explain Greedy Algorithm.

Answer:

Greedy Algorithms find the most optimized solutions bit by bit. The entire problem is divided into small steps and at each step the most optimal solution is taken which is then used in the next step, eliminating the other irrelevant solutions. The sum total of all optimal solutions is bound to be optimal too. It is the most preferred solution if it is feasible for a given problem. For finding the shortest path or minimum spanning tree problems, the greedy algorithm is the best. But it cannot be used in all cases, particularly when you are dealing with unsorted information.

140: Give some examples of Greedy Algorithm.

Answer:

The Greedy Algorithm is best used when we need an optimal solution under the given circumstances. But in certain cases, it cannot be used. Here are some situations which are best solved using the Greedy Algorithm:

a) **Kruksal's Minimum Spanning Tree** – Kruskal's Minimal Spanning tree requires us to find the path that costs minimum to traverse through all the vertices in the graph. For this the edges are ordered in the increasing order of their weight. The smallest edge is taken, checked for cycle, if found not cyclic, it is added to the tree or else discarded. This step is repeated until there's x-1 edges in the spanning tree, where x is the number of vertices.

b) **Prim's Minimal Spanning Tree** – Prim's Minimal Spanning Tree works such that, one of the vertices is chosen as the base, inserted into a new tree and all its edges are considered for weightage. The edge with the minimal weigtage is chosen and the rest are discarded from the tree. Its adjacent vertex is now considered and inserted into the new tree. Now this becomes the base vertex and the steps are repeated until a network spanning all the vertices are established.

141: Explain Iterative Algorithm.

Answer:

Iterative Algorithm uses iteration or loops and repeats a set of processes in the loop for each iteration value. It is different from recursion since recursion is calling the same function within its body and executing it until a particular condition is met. Here, number of iterations cannot be determined. Whereas in iteration, the number of times it repeats can be mentioned. Iterative algorithms are easier to implement and takes less memory compared to the other algorithms. Different kinds of loops are used for iterative algorithms.

142: Explain Algorithm analysis.

Answer:

Algorithm analysis is performed to check for the performance and complexity of multiple algorithms that can be used to solve the same problem. Two major factors that are considered for the analysis are time and space required to process the particular algorithm. Different algorithms are checked for these 2 factors with same values to decide on the most feasible algorithm that can be used. Based on the impending problem, if it is time sensitive, the fastest or the most optimal algorithm is considered. Similarly, for a space sensitive problem, the least space-occupying algorithm or the most optimal one is considered.

143: Explain Asymptotic Algorithm Analysis.

Answer:

When we frame the run-time performance matrix of an algorithm and choose the algorithm that performs in sync with the measurements expected, it is known as Asymptotic Algorithm. Here the best case, average case and worst case values are denoted as $O(n)$, $\Omega(n)$ or $\Theta(n)$ respectively. Each algorithm is analysed against these three cases with mathematical binding of the execution instead of considering the best or most optimal of the three. Once we have completed the Asymptotic Algorithm, we will have the clear information on the impending best, worst and average case scenarios.

144: Explain Tower of Hanoi.

Answer:

The Tower of Hanoi problem has a tower with more than 2 disks arranged in the order of the largest disk in the bottom to the smallest disk on the top. Moving only the topmost disk, one at a time, we have to rearrange the disks in the same order in another tower. The rule is that a large disk cannot stay on top of a small disk. This is best done using recursion.

a) We need 3 towers to start with. One which is the origin, one which is the destination and the third one is the temp one used for transit.

b) Start a function which will be recursively called which will take in 4 arguments, the origin, destination, transit and particular disk to be moved. It always starts with the n-1th disk.

c) For the first disk, if disk = 0, move it from origin to destination

d) Else

    i) Call the function recursively with disk -1, source remains the same, destination is now transit and transit is the destination. This moves the next topmost disk from source to transit

    ii) Move the topmost disk in source to destination

    iii) Call the function again with disk -1, transit is the source now, destination and source is the transit now. This moves the next topmost disk from transit to destination

e) Suppose we have 3 disks to move

f) Source, destination and transit arrays are defined. Source has the values {4, 3, 2}

g) First time, since we started from the topmost disk, disk to be moved is 2

h) So TOH is called with 2, Source, transit, destination
It calls TOH with 1, Source, destination, transit, which calls TOH with 0, Source, transit, destination

i) After the first pass, move the topmost disk in the source to destination

j) Then TOH is called with 2, transit, destination, source
It calls TOH with 1, transit, source, destination which calls TOH with 0, transit, destination, source

k) What actually happens is 2 goes into destination, 3 goes into transit

l) Then 2 goes from destination to transit

m) Then 4 goes from source to destination

n) Then 2 goes from transit to source

o) Then 3 goes from transit to destination

p) And finally, 2 goes from source to destination

145: Explain the algorithm for finding Fibonacci series.

Answer:

The Fibonacci series goes like this – 0 1 1 2 3 5 8 13 ... except for the first 2 numbers, the rest of them are all arrived at by adding the previous 2 numbers of the series.

To print the Fibonacci series,

We need a few variables such as firstNum, secondNum, nextNum, and counter

X is the user input to determine the number of terms in the series we need to print.

firstNum = 0

secondNum = 1

nextNum = 0

For (counter = 0; counter <= X; counter++)

Check for the first 2 numbers, since the calculations start after that only. So if counter <= 1,

nextNum = counter

Otherwise, take the previous 2 numbers and add them

nextNum = firstNum + secondNum

firstNum = secondNum

secondNum = nextNum

    print nextNum

  if x is input as 10,
For (counter = 0; counter <= 10; counter++)
    if counter <= 1,
        nextNum = counter
    else
        nextNum = firstNum + secondNum
        firstNum = secondNum
        secondNum = nextNum

    print nextNum

When counter = 0, nextNum = 0, so 0 is printed
When counter = 1, nextNum = 1, so 1 is printed
When counter = 2,
    nextNum = 0 + 1 = 1
    firstNum = 1
    secondNum = 1
    so 1 is printed
When counter = 3,
    nextNum = 1 + 1 = 2
    firstNum = 1
    secondNum = 2
    so 2 is printed
When counter = 4,
    nextNum = 1 + 2 = 3

firstNum = 2

secondNum = 3

so 3 is printed

When counter = 5,

    nextNum = 2 + 3 = 5

    firstNum = 3

    secondNum = 5

    so 5 is printed

When counter = 6,

    nextNum = 3 + 5 = 8

    firstNum = 5

    secondNum = 8

    so 8 is printed

When counter = 7,

    nextNum = 5 + 8 = 13

    firstNum = 8

    secondNum = 13

    so 13 is printed

When counter = 8,

    nextNum = 8 + 13 = 21

    firstNum = 13

    secondNum = 21

    so 21 is printed

When counter = 9,

    nextNum = 13 + 21 = 34

    firstNum = 21

    secondNum = 34

so 34 is printed

When counter = 10,

nextNum = 21 + 34 = 55

firstNum = 34

secondNum = 55

so 55 is printed

So the output is 0 1 1 2 3 5 8 13 21 34 55

146: Explain the algorithm for Sieve of Eratosthenes.

Answer:

The Sieve of Eratosthenes is in simple terms to print the prime numbers <= x, where x is the user input.

a) To do this first we have to consider all the numbers from 2 to x since 2 is the smallest prime number. We can create a list with these numbers for reference.

b) Create a Bit array of the same size which we will use to mark the corresponding numbers as prime or not. We have to initially mark all the elements as true.

c) Initialize a loop with primeNum = 2; primeNum* primeNum <= x; primeNum++

   i) Inside the loop, check if primeArr[primeNum] is true

      1. If true, initialize another loop with innerLoop = primeNum*2; innerLoop<=x; innerLoop += primeNum. This loop checks for all multiples of each number in the outer loop.

a. In this inner loop, mark primeArr[innerLoop] = false, since these are the multiples of another number and hence are not prime.

The inner loop will run for each and every number in the outer loop, which means all numbers from 2 till we reach the square root of the input number.

d) Once out of the outer loop, you can take another loop for the array and print all indices where the bit has been marked as primeArr[index] = true.

If x is input as 10,

Bool primeArr[10] is initialized with all values as true

For (primeNum = 2; primeNum* primeNum <= x; primeNum++)

 if primeArr[primeNum] is true

  For (innerLoop = primeNum * 2; innerLoop <= x; innerLoop += primeNum)

  Set primeArr[innerLoop] = false

First time, primeNum = 2, primeArr[2] is true

 For (innerLoop = 4; innerLoop <= 10; innerLoop += 2)

  primeArr[4] = false

  primeArr[6] = false

  primeArr[8] = false

  primeArr[10] = false

Next time primeNum = 3, primeArr[3] is true

    For (innerLoop = 6; innerLoop <= 10; innerLoop += 3)

        primeArr[6] = false

        primeArr[9] = false

Next time primeNum = 4, but primeArr[4] is set to false since it is a multiple of 2. So this step is skipped.

Next time primeNum = 5, primeArr[5] is true

    For (innerLoop = 10; innerLoop <= 10; innerLoop += 5)

        primeArr[10] = false

Finally, once out of the loop, take another loop

For (primeNum = 2; primeNum <= 10; primeNum++)

    If primeArr[primeNum] = true then print primeNum

    primeArr[2] = true so print 2

    primeArr[3] = true so print 3

    primeArr[4] = false so skip to the next iteration in loop

    primeArr[5] = true so print 5

    primeArr[6] = false so skip to the next iteration in loop

    primeArr[7] = true so print 7

    primeArr[8] = false so skip to the next iteration in loop

    primeArr[9] = false so skip to the next iteration in loop

    primeArr[10] = false so skip to the next iteration in loop

So the output is 2, 3, 5, and 7 which are the prime numbers less than 10.

147: Explain the algorithm for generating a random password of fixed length.

Answer:

a) Create a function which generates the password. The function will take in the length of the password.

b) Inside the function, declare and assign a string, say strChars, with all possible alpha-numeric characters that can be a part of the password. Typically password contains the alphabets in small and capital letters and all digits.

c) Store the length of the string into another variable say lenStrChars

d) Have another empty string variable strRandPWD to store the randomly created password

e) Start a loop that runs through the length of password required (as passed to the function from main)

f) Within the loop, take random characters from the string strChars (the string with all possible values) and push it into the desired password string strRandPWD. Take rand() % lenStrChars to make sure the array index stays below lenStrChars or the length of the string.

g) Once out of the loop, return strRandPWD

h) The main function will call this function with the number of digits' password it wants to generate.

148: Write the algorithm to check whether the given number is fancy.

Answer:

A fancy number mirrors itself. Examples of fancy numbers are 69, 88, 818 etc.

a) The magic digits are stored in a map with its index as the digit and its mirror as the value.

b) The map is stored as

mapVal['0'] = '0'

mapVal['1'] = '1'

mapVal['6'] = '9'

mapVal['8'] = '8'

mapVal['9'] = '6'

c) Further, the basic palindrome check is done with 2 counters, one that starts from the beginning and another that starts from the end.

d) A flag is set to true.

e) B starts from the beginning and E starts from the end.

f) Check if Arr[B] corresponds to any of the mapValues and whether Arr[E] corresponds to its value in mapValues. If it does not, set the flag to false and exit the loop otherwise continue this check till B<=E.

g) B++ and E-- are done in the loop

h) Once outside the loop, if the flag is true, it is a magic number, or else, it is not.

149: Write the algorithm to check whether the given number is Palindrome.

Answer:

A palindrome number is one that reads the same from left to right and right to left. For example 121, 13531, 2882 etc are palindrome numbers. The easiest way to check whether a number is a palindrome or not, is to reverse the number and check whether it is the same as the original number. For Palindromes, the number will be equal to the reversed number. It can be done using a recursive function.

a) Create a function that takes in 2 numbers, the number to be checked and the same stored in a pointer variable. This makes sure that every time the function is called recursively, a different number is passed as the base number while the duplicate number remains the same, being the pointer.

b) Check whether the first digit of the number is equal to the last digit of the number. The last digit of the number can be retrieved by using the mod or % operator. x % 10 will give the last digit of x.

c) Otherwise, check if the function recursively with the number n/10 and its duplicate's pointer returns true. If it returns false, return false and exit the function.

d) Change the duplicate's value to duplicate/10.

e) As the last step check whether x % 10 is equal to the value of duplicate pointer % 10 and return the result (true or false).

If the number is 12421, in the first pass

X = 12421 and *Y = 12421

Step 2 – is skipped until x becomes a single digit number. When x is a single digit, it checks whether x = Y%10 and returns the value true or false. In the last function call, the value becomes false and the recursion is exited.

Step 3 – isPalNum (1242, Y) -> isPalNum (124, Y) -> isPalNum (12, Y) -> isPalNum (1, Y)

At this stage - isPalNum (1, Y), Step 2 is called which gives true.

So isPalNum (12, Y) is executed.

Step 4 – Y = Y/10 = 1242.

Step 5 – x % 10 = 2, Y % 10 = 2. So return true.

Now isPalNum (124, Y) is executed

Step 4 – Y = Y/10 = 124.

Step 5 – x % 10 = 4, Y % 10 = 4. So return true.

Now isPalNum (1242, Y) is executed

Step 4 – Y = Y/10 = 12.

Step 5 – x % 10 = 2, Y % 10 = 2. So return true.

Now isPalNum (12421, Y) is executed

Step 4 – Y = Y/10 = 1.

Step 5 – x % 10 = 1, Y % 10 = 1. So return true.

Finally, at Step 2, the recursion is exited.

150: Write the algorithm to reverse an array.

Answer:

To reverse an array, the method is simple.

Have 2 counter variables

The string array is bsArr

One counter variable will start from the beginning, cntBeg and count up. The other will start from the end, cntEnd and count down.

Set cntEnd = length of the array - 1

In a loop cntBeg = 0; cntBeg < cntEnd; cntBeg++,

    swap the array elements

    tmpVal = bsArr[cntBeg]

    bsArr[cntBeg] = bsArr[cntEnd];

    bsArr[cntEnd] = tmpVal;

    cntEnd--;

End of the loop will be when it comes to the middle of the array.

If bsArr[] = {11, 12, 13, 14, 15},

    cntBeg = 0

    cntEnd = 4

    cntBeg = 0; cntBeg < cntEnd; cntBeg++,

First Pass

    tmpVal = bsArr[0], tmpVal = 11

    bsArr[0] = bsArr[4], bsArr[0] = 15

    bsArr[4] = 11, bsArr[4] = 11

    cntEnd--; cntEnd = 3

Second Pass

    tmpVal = bsArr[1], tmpVal = 12

    bsArr[1] = bsArr[3], bsArr[1] = 14

    bsArr[3] = 11, bsArr[3] = 11

cntEnd--; cntEnd = 2

Third Pass does not clear since cntBeg = 2 and cndEnd = 2.

So the reversed array is bsArr[] = {15, 14, 13, 12, 11}.

Chapter 11

Sorting Algorithms

151: How do you classify sorting algorithms?

Answer:

Sorting algorithms can be broadly classified comparison based & counting based, and in-place & not-in-place algorithms. Most of the sorting algorithms are based on comparison. The basic idea is to compare 2 elements and swap them or rearrange them based on the particular type of algorithm used. Examples of comparison based algorithms are bubble sort, heap sort, selection sort, quick sort etc. The counting based algorithms like bucket sort and radix sort use the divide and rule algorithms to divide the entire collection and then sort the elements. The in-place algorithms are carried out without using any additional array or data structure. Examples of in-place algorithms are quick sort and heap sort. The not-in-place algorithms use an additional array or data structure for sorting. Examples of not-in-place algorithms are bucket sort and merge sort.

152: What are some of the popular sorting algorithms?

Answer:

Sorting can be done using various algorithms based on the collection or data structure to be sorted. The popular sorting algorithms can be categorized as simple sorts, efficient sorts, distribution sorts and variants of bubble sort. Simple sorts are done for small data. Efficient sorts perform better than simple sorts but are not quite efficient when it comes to large volume of data. But they work well with random collections. Bubble sort and its variants are highly inefficient and are used only for training purposes. Distribution sorts make use of multiple resources to distribute the source data for sorting and then finally come with the sorted data in the source.

153: Explain the different techniques used for sorting?

Answer:

The commonly used sorting techniques are stable & non-stable, adaptive & non-adaptive and in-place and not-in-place algorithms. Stable algorithms are those that never change the order in which similar elements are available in the source. Non-stable algorithms are those that change the order in which similar elements are taken. Adaptive algorithm considers the already ordered elements and does not bother much about them. But non-adaptive algorithms never bother whether an element is already ordered or not. It just follows the sorting over and again till all the elements are sorted. In-place algorithms do not make use of additional arrays or data structures for sorting, whereas, the not-in-place algorithms use temporary array or data structure to store the values being sorted temporarily.

154: What are stable and non-stable sorting algorithms?

Answer:

Stable algorithms do not change the order of the similar elements in the source. They appear in the same order even after sorting. Non-stable or unstable sorting algorithm changes the order in which similar elements appear in the original source. For example,

Unsorted

0	1	2	3	4
14	44	44	12	9

Sorted with Stable algorithm

0	1	2	3	4
44	44	14	12	9

Unsorted

0	1	2	3	4
14	44	44	12	9

Sorted with unstable algorithm

0	1	2	3	4
44	44	14	12	9

155: What are adaptive and non-adaptive sorting algorithms?

Answer:

Adaptive algorithms check for already sorted elements in the source and just use them as they are in the destination. If in a list of elements to be sorted, if the adaptive algorithm finds some elements that are already sorted, it does not attempt a sort on these elements and just use the already sorted elements instead. Timsort, patience sort and smoothsort are examples of adaptive sorting algorithms. Non-adaptive algorithms try to sort the already sorted elements also along with the rest of the elements. They re-order every single element to make sure that the array is completely sorted. Bubble sort is a popularly known non-adaptive sorting algorithm.

156: How do you check for stability in sorting algorithms?

Answer:

Any sorting algorithm can be made stable by making sure that the equal keys are coming in the same order as before sorting. While checking for the stability in the sorting algorithm being used, multiple conditions are checked that includes its keys before and after sorting. If you have a set of elements that are identical but appear more than once in a list, if their order is maintained after the sort is completed, it is said to be a stable sorting algorithm.

157: Explain Insertion Sort.

Answer:

Insertion Sort is an in-place sorting algorithm where sorting happens during insertion itself as the name suggests. Whenever a new element in being input, it checks for its position in the list or array and inserts the element in the appropriate position so that the array remains sorted even after insertion.

a) The first element (e1) is compared with the next element (e2) and swapped. If e1 > e2, then e2 becomes the first element and e1 becomes the 2nd.

b) The above step is repeated with the next 2 elements – the second (e1) and the third (e3). If e1 > e3, e3 becomes the 2nd element and e1 becomes 3rd.

c) Now before moving on with the next element, the ordered subarray is checked again. If e2 > e3, they are swapped. So e3 is the 1st element, e2 is the 2nd element

d) Every 2 adjacent elements are compared and swapped and for each swap into the subarray of ordered list within the array, they are further compared and swapped so that at any given point of time, the subarray in the beginning will always have the sorted list.

158: Explain Selection Sort.

Answer:

Selection sort is probably the simplest sorting method to understand. The given list is divided into 2 and one part contains the sorted elements and the other contains the unsorted elements. As the sorting algorithm progresses, the sorted part gets longer and the unsorted gets smaller since the elements from the unsorted part are added to the sorted part till eventually the entire array is sorted.

a) The smallest element is extracted from the array and inserted into the first position.

b) Now the array to be considered for sorting is considered from the second position and the first step is repeated.

c) Every time the sorted array gets a new element and the unsorted array shrinks by one element.

d) This continues till there is no element in the unsorted section.

159: What are the efficient sort algorithms used and why?

Answer:

Merge sort, heap sort and quick sort are considered as efficient sorting algorithms. Of these, quick sort is considered one of the most efficient sorting algorithms. The efficiency is decided usually based on 4 factors – implementation, performance, memory used and time complexity. While they all perform well with random data, for real-time implementations, variations of these algorithms are used. Sometimes even a combination of these algorithms are used so that one's efficiency or memory management and the other one's time complexity are maximum utilized, and you get a more efficient algorithm with the best of all the algorithms used.

160: Explain Merge sort.

Answer:

Merge sort works based on the divide and conquer technique. The basic idea is to divide the entire data into smallest units possible and work on them for sorting and then merge them again to form the sorted array. If we have an array of 6 elements – {6, 3, 1, 14, 2, 10}, it is split into 6 elements, step by step and then sorted and merged step by step until it forms the ordered array {1, 2, 3, 6, 10, 14}. In each step, the elements are sorted first and then merged, as illustrated below:

{6, 3, 1, 14, 2, 10}
{6, 3, 1} {14, 2, 10}
{6, 3} {1, 14} {2, 10}

{6} {3} {1} {14} {2} {10}

{3, 6} {1, 14} {2, 10}
{1, 3, 6} {2, 10, 14}
{1, 2, 3, 6, 10, 14}

161: Explain Heapsort.

Answer:

Heapsort is somewhat like the selection sort. In heap sort, the largest element from the list is taken first and moved to the last position of the array or the heap. The rest of the elements are considered in the unsorted heap. The largest element in the unsorted heap becomes the second last element of the sorted heap. The previous 2 steps are repeated until the unsorted heap has no elements.

For this unsorted array

{6, 3, 1, 14, 2, 10}

Heap sort will be

{6, 3, 1, 2, 10}{14} (It is in the same array only)

{6, 3, 1, 2}{10, 14}

{3, 1, 2}{6, 10, 14}

{1, 2}{3, 6, 10, 14}

{1}{2, 3, 6, 10, 14}

{1, 2, 3, 6, 10, 14} – Sorted Array

162: Explain Quicksort.

Answer:

Quicksort is considered as the most efficient sorting algorithm. To implement quicksort, recursive functions are used. The logic used for recursion is simple.

a) The rightmost element is considered as a pivot and the array is divided into 2 – one with elements less than the pivot and the other with elements greater than the pivot.

b) Now get the pivot in between.

For each partition repeat steps a & b.

To sort the array {6, 3, 1, 14, 2, 10} using quicksort, 10 is the pivot since it is the rightmost element.

{6, 3, 1, 14, 2} {10}

{6, 3, 1, 2} {10} {14}

{6, 3, 1} {2} (pivot) {10} {14}

{1} {2} {6, 3} {10} {14}

{1} {2} {6} {3} (pivot) {10} {14}

{1} {2} {3} {6} {10} {14}

{1, 2, 3, 6, 10, 14}

163: Explain Bubble sort.

Answer:

Bubble sort is probably one of the most uneconomical sort algorithms even though it is the easiest to comprehend and employ. It uses the compare and exchange method till the entire array is sorted.

To sort this array {8, 4, 1, 24, 2, 20} using Bubble Sort

{8, 4, 1, 24, 2, 20} -> {4, 8, 1, 24, 2, 20} - > {4, 1, 8, 24, 2, 20} -> {4, 1, 8, 24, 2, 20} -> {4, 1, 8, 2, 24, 20} -> {4, 1, 8, 2, 20, 24}

{4, 1, 8, 2, 20, 24} -> {1, 4, 8, 2, 20, 24} -> {1, 4, 8, 2, 20, 24} -> {1, 4, 2, 8, 20, 24} -> {1, 4, 2, 8, 20, 24} -> {1, 4, 2, 8, 20, 24}

{1, 4, 2, 8, 20, 24} -> {1, 4, 2, 8, 20, 24} -> {1, 2, 4, 8, 20, 24} -> {1, 2, 4, 8, 20, 24} -> {1, 2, 4, 8, 20, 24} -> {1, 2, 4, 8, 20, 24}

{1, 2, 4, 8, 20, 24} -> {1, 2, 4, 8, 20, 24} -> {1, 2, 4, 8, 20, 24} -> {1, 2, 4, 8, 20, 24} -> {1, 2, 4, 8, 20, 24}

In the last round, when the array became {1, 2, 4, 8, 20, 24}, since there was no swapping done, the Bubble sort process is considered complete.

164: Explain Shell sort.

Answer:

Shell sort is considered a very professional sorting technique. It is similar to insertion sort. The main difference here is that instead of considering extreme shifts or arrays involving a large number of elements, an interval is chosen. So instead of choosing elements on 2 extreme ends, elements with this interval x are chosen to compare and sort.

To sort this array {6, 3, 1, 14, 2, 10} using Shell Sort

Interval = 3

These pairs have to be sorted {6, 14} {3, 2} {1, 10}

Now the array becomes {6, 14, 2, 3, 1, 10}

Now with Interval = 2, these 2 arrays have to be sorted {6, 2, 1} {14, 3, 10}

Now the array becomes {1, 2, 6, 3, 10, 14}

Now with Interval = 1

The array becomes {1, 2, 3, 6, 10, 14}

165: Explain Comb sort.

Answer:

Comb sort is a combination of shell sort and bubble sort. In comb sort, the interval diminishes by 1.25 for each pass. Bubble sort is carried out for each pass until nothing is swapped.

The interval or gap is initially the size of the array.

The outer loop checks for gap = 1 and swapflag = 0 (for bubble sort)

Within this loop, gap is diminished

gap = gap / 1.25

Make sure that gap = 1 in case it goes below that.

Set the swapflag to 0, counter2 to 0

Start the next loop until (counter2 + gap) >= size of array

Check and swap array[counter2] and array[counter2 + gap]

Set swapflag to 1 if swapped

Increment counter2 by 1

End of inner loop

End of outer loop

166: What are the various distribution sort algorithms used?

Answer:

For distribution sort, the logic applied is to move the data temporarily to other arrays, sort them and then populate the original array with the sorted data. Distribution sort is particularly useful when dealing with large volumes of data. There are 2 phases in distribution sorting. In the first phase, a chunk of data small enough to fit in the computer's memory is accessed; it is then sorted and kept in the storage disk temporarily. In the second phase these smaller chunks of sorted data are merged into the sorted array. The sort phase may be done using quicksort or any other feasible sort algorithm.

167: Explain Counting sort.

Answer:

Counting sort is used when you have to sort a range of values. To sort this range, an index array is created in which the occurrence of each value within the range is recorded. This index array is used to populate the actual array with fresh sorted values. For example, if the array is within the range 1 to 8 and the has values {3, 4, 1, 7, 5, 4, 1, 4, 3}

tempArr[]

0	1	2	3	4	5	6	7	8
0	2	0	2	3	1	0	1	0

Sorted Array

0	1	2	3	4	5	6	7	8
1	1	3	3	4	4	4	5	7

168: Explain Bucket sort.

Answer:

Bucket sort can be considered an extension of counting sort. Instead of storing the number of occurrences for each number, for each index or range, a bucket array is created with the sorted values.

Array to be sorted {124, 114, 105, 134, 125, 137, 121, 145, 178, 141, 168, 122}

Because the numbers can be classified as between 100 and 200 and those with 0 to 7 in tenth's place,

0	{105}
1	{114}
2	{121, 122, 124, 125}
3	{134, 137}
4	{141, 145}
5	
6	{168}
7	{178}

Finally, the buckets are inserted into an array in the same order which will be the sorted array

{105, 114, 121, 122, 124, 125, 134, 137, 141, 145, 168, 178}

169: Explain Radix sort.

Answer:

Radix sort is a combination of comparison sort and counting sort. It sorts the numbers given one digit at a time starting from the unit's place working up to the uppermost digit's place value. If the array to be sorted {124, 114, 105, 134, 125, 137, 121, 145, 178, 241, 168, 122} it first sorts the numbers based on the digit in the unit's place. For more than 1 number with the same digit in the unit's place, it retains the number's position in the array.

1-> {124, 114, 105, 134, 125, 137, 121, 145, 178, 241, 168, 122}

2-> {121, 241, 122, 124, 114, 134, 105, 125, 145, 137, 178, 168}

Now the next digit's place value is taken, 10's place

3-> {121, 241, 122, 124, 114, 134, 105, 125, 145, 137, 178, 168}

4-> {105, 114, 121, 122, 124, 125, 134, 137, 241, 145, 168, 178}

Now the next digit's place value is taken, 100's place

5-> {105, 114, 121, 122, 124, 125, 134, 137, 241, 145, 168, 178}

6-> {105, 114, 121, 122, 124, 125, 134, 137, 145, 168, 178, 241}

The array is sorted.

170: What do you mean by index sorting?

Answer:

Index sorting is done for very large data when it cannot be loaded into the computer's memory for sorting. This is especially useful when we are dealing with heavy database records or arrays of complex data structure. If the information is unique, it can be indexed otherwise and then sorted based on the index. This way, the full table or the data need not be loaded for sorting. Instead, the unique indices can be loaded into another table and they can be sorted. Once the indices are sorted, the table can be accessed based on these keys in the sorted order.

171: Explain Pigeonhole Sort.

Answer:

Pigeonhole sort is very much like the bucket sort. Key – value pairs of a particular range are considered for pigeonhole sort. For each key, an empty pigeonhole is created and all elements corresponding to that key is inserted into that pigeonhole in a sorted way. Finally, these pigeonholes are merged to get the sorted values.

{(2, "XScissors"), (1, "YBook"), (2, "ZPencils"), (3, "APens"), (1, "CBoard"), (5, "BPapers")}

Here the keys range between 1 and 5.

1	(1, "CBoard") (1, "YBook")
2	(2, "ZPencils") (2, "XScissors")
3	(3, "APens")
4	
5	(5, "BPapers")

The sorted list would be {(1, "CBoard"), (1, "YBook"), (2, "ZPencils"), (2, "XScissors"), (3, "APens"), (5, "BPapers")}

172: Explain some of the issues faced for implementation of quicksort.

Answer:

Even though Quicksort is considered the most efficient sort algorithm, there are some implementation issues that work against using the quicksort algorithm. The first issue is that with repeated elements. Quicksort does not work well with a lot of repeated elements. When we reach a point where one of the partitions remain empty and the other one has the same elements repeated. Even with the same numbers, the sorting happens one by one which is a total waste of resources. Choosing the pivot is another major issue with quicksort. Even though most of the algorithms use the last indexed element, ideally, the recursive median of 3 should be the pivot. There are multiple optimization methods and choosing between them is also complicated. Since quicksort implements the divide and conquer method, it is not very scalable when compared to some other algorithms in use.

173: What do you mean by shuffling?

Answer:

Shuffling is randomly rearranging a deck of cards based on the random numbers picked by the computer. Shuffling works just to the opposite of sorting. While sorting, you have an unordered array which you sort and make in an order. In shuffling, you do the opposite; make a deck of cards that's ordered into a set of unordered elements. Different algorithms can be used for shuffling. This algorithm is used for online gambling and for card games. Each card is assigned an index and form a random permutation from these numbers. Arrange the cards in the order of their shuffled indices. These permutations and combinations have to keep changing randomly for online gambling and card games to be successful.

174: Explain Cycle Sort.

Answer:

Cycle sort works only with known array values. The idea is to trace the first or lowest element and work around it.

For example, take the array {11, 7, 2, 4, 6}

{11, 7, 2, 4, 6}

Its sorted form is {2, 4, 6, 7, 11}

It can be considered as a cycle forward of elements 2, 4 and 6 that are already sorted and then a swap of 7 and 11.

The first step would be {2, 4, 6, 11, 7}

And the second step would be {2, 4, 6, 7, 11}

But this will not be possible in all cases with different elements. But in such a case, where the array is partly sorted, the sorting is complete in 2 writes.

175: Explain sorted insert into a singly linked list.

Answer:

The idea is to insert into an already sorted singly linked list such that the newly inserted element adheres to the sort. To effect this, the position has to be searched and marked first and then the new element has to be inserted. While inserting a new node, the links also have to be maintained. Once the position of the new node is marked, the current element in that position has to point to this node and the current element's next should be the new node's next. Once these are effected, the new node is successfully inserted into the sorted position.

Linked List

5	10	15	20	25	30

The amount to be inserted is 22

So it has to be inserted between 20 and 25.

5	10	15	20	22	25	30

For this, 20's next is stored in 22nd's next pointer. 20 will now point to 22. So 20 will point to 22, 22 will point to 25.

176: Which algorithms takes minimum number of memory writes and why?

Answer:

The cycle sort takes the minimum number of writes. It is because part of the source array is already sorted and another part of it requires only swapping. In cycle sort, the part of the array that's already sorted is just forward cycled such that it is positioned corrected in the sorted array. More than often, very few other elements are left that are swapped. This requires minimal writes when compared to the usual algorithms that do not consider the already sorted items and explicitly sort them again.

177: Why is quick sort preferred for Arrays and merge sort for Linked lists?

Answer:

Quicksort is the most efficient in-place sorting algorithm. For an efficient quicksort using pointers, you will need 2 of them, one scanning from the beginning and the other scanning from the end and checking for values and swapping them. But when it comes to sequential data such as files, they allow only forward traversing. But with merge sort, it requires auxiliary space to store the data being sorted temporarily. When it comes to very large data, this temporary space may not be practical. But since linked lists contain pointers to the next element, they just need to handle the pointers and rest comes to them easily.

This page is intentionally left blank.

Chapter 12

Search Algorithms

178: Explain the algorithm for linear search.

Answer:

The linear search is the simplest of all search algorithms. The entire array is searched from the very first element till the element is found or till the end of array. The element is compared with all elements of the array till a match is found. Linear search can be done on a sorted or unsorted array.

179: Explain the algorithm for binary search.

Answer:

Binary search involves searching in a sorted array. The value to be searched is checked against the middle-most item of the array. If the middle element is equal to the search element, the element is found. Otherwise, if the element is less than the middle element, only the first half of the array is searched for. If the element is greater than the middle element, only the second half is searched. The steps are repeated until the entire array has been searched.

180: Explain interpolation search.

Answer:

Interpolation search is an extension of Binary search. It is similar to searching through an indexed array of information like the telephone directory which is sorted by name. As in the dictionary when we search for a name, we know that it is sorted and we always start within the known range of names to search. This narrows down the search to a manageable section from a large volume of data. As in binary search, we have already left out the section not to be searched and each time, we are narrowing down the search limit leaving the undesired pages as we search for a particular combination of alphabets only.

181: Write the algorithm to find the largest element in an array of unique elements

Answer:

To find the third largest element in an array, we can iterate through it and use the following algorithm:

intArr[] = {3, 1, 53, 33, 41, 10, 100}
The third largest number is 41.

We need 3 variables to store 3 numbers – so declare intSecond and intThird and initialize them to zero.

Since we start checking for values from the first element, we can assign intFirst = intArr[0]

We will start the iteration from the 2nd index of the array as we already have the first value with us.

For counterArr = 1; counterArr < intArr.size; counterArr++

    If intArr[counterArr] > intFirst

        intThird = intSecond

        intSecond = intFirst

        intFirst = intArr[counterArr]

    else if intArr[counterArr] > intSecond

        intThird = intSecond

        intSecond = intArr[counterArr]

    else if intArr[counterArr] > intThird

        intThird = intArr[counterArr]

Once the whole array is traversed, intThird will have the 3rd largest value which is 41.

intArr[] = {3, 1, 53, 33, 41, 10, 100}

intFirst = 3, intSecond = 0, intThird = 0

First Pass 1 < 3, so first condition is not satisfied,

    1 > 0, second condition is satisfied and hence,

intThird = 0, intSecond = 1

2nd pass 53 > 3, intThird = 1, intSecond = 3, intFirst = 53

3rd pass 33 < 53, but 33 > 3 intThird = 3, intSecond = 33

4th pass 41 < 53, but 41 > 33 intThird = 33, intSecond = 41

5th pass 10 < 41, Does not satisfy any condition

6th pass 100 > 41, intThird = 41, intSecond = 53, intFirst = 100

So at the end of the loop, intThird has the third largest value which is 41.

182: Write the algorithm to find the LCM of array elements

Answer:

To find the LCM of any 2 numbers, you can apply the formula

LCM(x, y) = (x * y) / GCD(x, y)

GCD is the greatest common divisor

So in an array, this formula has to be applied to every 2 adjacent numbers. To find the LCM of an array

intArr[] = {3, 5, 6, 8, 9}

arrSize = 5

We need a recursive function to find the GCD,

GCD (int x, int y)

    If y == 0

    return x

GCD(y, x%y)

To find the LCM,

lcm = intArr[0]

We use a loop

For counterLoop = 1; counterLoop<arrSize; counterLoop++

lcm = (lcm * intArr(counterLoop)) /

GCD(intArr(counterLoop), lcm)

By the end of the iteration, lcm will have the actual LCM of the array.

intArr[] = {3, 5, 6, 8, 9}

Pass	LCM before calculation	Calculation	GCD	LCM after calculation
First	3	(3 * 5) / gcd(5, 3)	1	15
Second	15	(15 * 6) / gcd(6, 15)	3	30
Third	30	(30 * 8) / gcd(8, 30)	2	120
Fourth	120	(120 * 9) / gcd(9, 120)	3	360

So lcm of {3, 5, 6, 8, 9} = 360.

183: Write the algorithm to find the position of an element in the given sorted array of infinite elements.

Answer:

To find a number from a sorted array, the Binary search algorithm can be used. But you need the upper and lower bounds of an array to search within. So the first job here is to find the bounds to search within. This is done by a simple logic

Within a loop, the array value is checked against the key to be searched. Since the array is sorted, we don't have to go beyond that key. So the lower and upper bounds are set within the loop as below:

intArr[] = {3, 5, 6, 8, 9}

lowerBound = 0

upperBound = 1

arrVal = intArr[0]

while arrVal < searchKey

     lowerBound = upperBound

     upperBound *= 2

     arrVal = intArr[upperBound]

Once outside this loop, we will have the lowerBound and upperBound for checking.

Using these bounds, a binary search on the array with the bounds for the key can be done.

intArr[] = {3, 5, 6, 8, 9}

Searching for 7

lowerBound = 0

upperBound = 1

arrVal = 3

Pass	arrVal (before)	lowerBound	upperBound	arrVal (new val)
First	3	0	1	6
Second	6	1	2	9

lowerBound = 2

upperBound = 4

The loop does not run beyond this and the binary search is done within the bounds 2 and 4 which do not yield the key.

Searching for 6

lowerBound = 0

upperBound = 1

arrVal = 3

Pass	arrVal (before)	lowerBound	upperBound	arrVal (new val)
First	3	0	1	6

lowerBound = 1

upperBound = 2

The loop does not run beyond this and the binary search is done within the bounds 1 and 2 and finds the key at index 2.

184: Write the algorithm to find how many times an element repeats in a sorted array.

Answer:

It can be done using a linear search or with binary search. Using linear search, just search for the key and every time the key is found, increment a counter. The logic is very simple, but takes longer time, when dealing with large volume of data.

Binary search is the better option to find the occurrences of a key in an array. Using binary search, first the first occurrence of the key is found. Then its last occurrence is found. The difference between the indices gives the number of times the key repeats in the sorted array.

The first occurrence can be easily found using binary search. To find the last occurrence, the lower bound for binary search is given as the index of the first occurrence plus 1 and upper bound is the size of the array.

If firstFound = first index where keyVal is found
lastFound = last index where keyVal is found
No. Of occurrences = lastFound − firstFound + 1

185: Explain the Graph BFS Algorithm.

Answer:

BFS or Breadth First Search Algorithm for graphs first

considers all the nodes in the same level and then only it traverses to the next level of nodes.

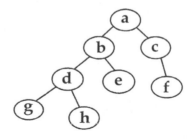

In BSF, a queue and a flag are used to mark each node visited while traversing.

Traversing starts with 'a' which is the root.

'a' is marked visited first.

From 'a' we move on to the first node in the next level which is 'b', mark it visited and enqueue it. Move to the next node 'c', mark it visited and enqueue it. Now the queue has b and c in it. Take out 'b' first and move to its child nodes 'd' and 'e', mark them visited, and enqueue them. Now the queue contains c, d, e. So the next element to visit is the 'c' node. This continues till the queue becomes empty and all the nodes are marked visited.

186: Explain the Graph DFS Algorithm.

Answer:

The DSF or Depth First Search algorithm implies that all the child nodes of a node, in different levels, are visited first and then moves on to the next node.

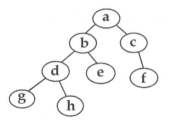

For the above graph, the traversal path in DFS would be a->b->d->g->->g->e->c->f

After each node-visit, that node is marked visited and added to a stack. When there are no more nodes to add in the stack, the last added element is popped out. The adjacent node of the popped out element which is not marked visited is visited next. The previous steps are repeated till all the nodes are marked visited. The traversal continues till the stack becomes empty.

187: Write the algorithm to check if the given array is a subset of another array, using Binary Search.

Answer:

To check whether an array is the subset of another binary array, a simple algorithm with 2 loops can be used. The outer loop checks for each element of smaller array which has to be checked for subset. For each element in the subset array, all the elements of the outer array or the bigger array is checked. If a match for an element in the subarray is found in the main array at any point, the inner loop breaks. Or else, the value of the counter of inner loop will equal the length of the array. So if the loop has worked throughout and a match is not found, it means, the 2nd array is not a subset.

For outerCounter = 0; outerCounter<sizeof(intArr2); outerCounter++

    For innerCounter = 0; innerCounter<sizeof(intArr1); innerCounter++

        If intArr2[outerCounter] == intArr1[innerCounter]

            Break the loop

      If outerCounter == sizeof(intArr1)

          Not found

intArr1[] = {1, 2, 3, 4, 5, 6}

intArr2[] = {2, 4, 5}

outer Counter	inner Counter	intArr1 [innerCounter]	intArr2 [outerCounter]	Outer Counter < 6
0	0	1	2	
	1	2	2	True
1	0	1	4	
	1	2	4	
	2	3	4	
	3	4	4	True
2	0	1	5	
	1	2	5	
	2	3	5	
	3	4	5	
	4	5	5	True

Since all the elements were found in the main array, intArr2 is a subset of intArr1.

188: How will you search in an almost sorted array?

Answer:

When we need to search in an almost sorted array, it means that the array is more or less sorted, except for a few elements here and there. So we can start searching for the key from the middle as usual. The only difference being, we search for the 3 middle numbers first and then decide on whether to continue with a binary search for left array or right array. The advantage of doing this is, when we consider 3 elements in the middle, we get an idea of how well sorted the array is. Sometimes the key to be searched is in the middle, or the very next elements before or after it, and the search ends with single pass. Otherwise, if the key is less than mid value, search the left subarray or else, search the right subarray with the same steps.

189: Explain why a Binary search is better than a Ternary search.

Answer:

A Binary search involves splitting the array into half and searching each half separately. A ternary search involves splitting the array into 3 parts and searching each separately. So when a binary search will involve 2 searches in each level, the ternary will involve 3 searches in each level. Technically, a binary search takes $\log2 (x) + O(1)$ comparisons to complete whereas a ternary search involves $2\log3 (x) + O(1)$ comparisons. This means that a ternary search will require more comparisons to search than a binary search and hence, binary search is a better option.

190: How can we check if the given tree is a binary heap?

Answer:

A tree is considered a binary heap, if the parent is always larger than its children throughout the tree. Even though there are many methods to check for this, the simplest to implement is the iterative method which is as follows:

Take a loop that runs through the tree elements till the last parent node.

Compare each node with its children, if the parent > child, if not, the tree is not a binary heap.

To effect this loop and checking:

For loopCounter = 0; loopCounter <= (arrSize-2)/2; loopCounter++

 Check for the left child

 If intArr[(2*loopCounter) + 1] > intArr[loopCounter]

  Not binary heap

 Check for right child

 If intArr[(2*loopCounter) + 2] > intArr[loopCounter]

  Not binary heap

This page is intentionally left blank.

Chapter 13

Huffman Coding

191: What is Huffman Coding?

Answer:

Huffman coding uses prefixes or weights to assign a code to the data being transmitted. More frequent codes get less weight and the rarely transmitted codes get more weight. These codes are bit sequences assigned to the data which makes it a unique stream of data which can be easily decoded by the receiver without any vagueness. The codes or bit strings are assigned based on their probability or occurrence in the stream. This involves building a Huffman tree from the given data and to traverse the tree to assign the bit streams to the data.

192: How do you generate a Huffman Tree from a given set of values?

Answer:

Building a Huffman tree is best explained with an example:

Given a set of values and their frequencies

Value	Frequency
2	8
4	12
6	15
8	25
10	30

The data is sorted by frequency and the lowest 2 frequencies are made the child nodes and add them up to make the parent node.

8:2 and 12:4 are the child nodes and 20:* is the parent node

Add this to the list removing the 2 child nodes. Now we get the new list sorted by frequency as

Value	Frequency
6	15
*	20
8	25
10	30

Now add the parent node 35:* with child nodes 15:6 and 20:*.

Add this to the list removing the 2 child nodes. Now we get the new list sorted by frequency as

Value	Frequency
8	25
10	30
*	35

Now add the parent node 55:* with child nodes 25:8 and 30:10. Add this to the list removing the 2 child nodes. Now we get the new list sorted by frequency as

Value	Frequency
*	35
*	55

Now add the parent node 90:* with child nodes 35:* and 55:*. Add this to the list removing the 2 child nodes. Now we get the new list sorted by frequency as

Value	Frequency
*	90

Now with this list we can create the Huffman Tree

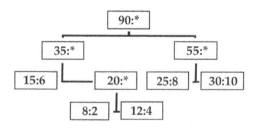

193: What are the techniques used in Huffman Coding?

Answer:

Huffman coding involves Compression and Decompression of data using binary codes. Compression is the process of creating the binary trees based on their probability in the series. Based on the position on the tree, each node or element is given a binary series that makes it unique to the sender. Assuming that the sender has the tree, he can build the data based on the code received, plotting it on the tree. This technique is called decompression or decoding. The same can be done using look up tables also.

194: Explain Compression technique for Huffman Coding.

Answer:

Compression is the process by which the elements are plotted on a binary tree formed with their frequency in the series. The entire data is sorted based on its probability or frequency and this information is used to create a binary tree as detailed earlier. This binary tree is called the Huffman Tree. Now each element in the tree is prefixed with a binary code based on its position in the tree which makes the code unique since at one position there's only one element. Huffman tree can be created in top-down or bottom-up method.

195: Explain Decompression technique for Huffman Coding.

Answer:

Decompression or decoding the elements in Huffman coding

assumes that the receiver has access to the Huffman tree created by the sender. Huffman coding – decoding works such that the coding map is shared between the sender and the receiver. The stream bit is decoded and used to traverse the tree till a leaf is reached. Once the leaf or the position is traced, the symbol or data is mapped there. Similarly, all the streams are mapped in the tree and the corresponding symbols or data are mapped forming the binary map.

196: What are the main properties of Huffman Coding?

Answer:

In Huffman Coding we consider the frequencies of the symbols for plotting them in the Huffman Tree. These frequencies can be either actual frequencies or generic probabilities arrived upon based on the average actual experiences. This has to be available with the symbol to be decoded. Huffman coding works more efficiently with longer symbols or words than with single characters.

197: What are the variations of Huffman Coding available?

Answer:

There are many implementations of Huffman coding popularly in use. Some of them are n-ary Huffman coding, Huffman template algorithm, Adaptive Huffman coding, Huffman coding with unequal letter costs, Length-limited Huffman coding, canonical Huffman code and optimal alphabetic binary trees or Hu–Tucker coding. While some of them use Huffman-like algorithms for coding and decoding, some others have totally different considerations for the prefixes. For example, the n-ary Huffman coding uses a range between {0, 1, .., n-1} alphabets to encode instead of the binaries. The Adaptive Huffman coding technique uses the probabilities calculated based on the actual frequencies available, even though it works slower.

198: Explain Huffman Template Algorithm.

Answer:

in Huffman coding, the frequencies are usually used as weights to encode the symbols or data. In Huffman Template Algorithm, we can use any weight or combination of weights that forms the basis of sorting. Weight can be cost, occurrence, or any other weight which can even be non-numerical. The only requirement is that the symbol needs to be weighted. Such implementations tend to solve some minimization problems that usually comes up during encoding.

199: Explain Adaptive Huffman coding.

Answer:

Adaptive Huffman Coding or Dynamic Huffman coding builds the prefix code dynamically as they are being sent. There's no pre-planned tree mapping available for this type of Huffman coding implementation. Many algorithms are used to implement Adaptive Huffman coding such as Vitter Algorithm and FGK Algorithm. In Vitter Algorithm, the nodes are numbered based on their position on the tree. The leaf nodes get lower numbers while the upper nodes get higher numbers. The highest numbered node is the leader of a block. A block is formed by many leaves or nodes of the same type and weight put together. The FGK Algorithm or the Faller-Gallager-Knuth Algorithm is implemented by dynamically adding the incoming node into the Huffman tree. This involved considerable number of swapping of subtrees or nodes or leaves. The Vitter algorithm was developed to improvise on this.

200: What are the applications of Huffman Coding?

Answer:

Huffman coding is used for coding and decoding information. Arithmetic coding is a standard implementation of Huffman coding. Arithmetic coding, in fact, is a better implementation since it includes alphabets and numbers for coding as against the binary coding implemented by Huffman coding. Huffman coding is used as a backend to widely used encoding methods. Multimedia codecs such as MP3s and JPEGs use Huffman coding along with other methods.

This page is intentionally left blank.

HR Questions

Review these typical interview questions and think about how you would answer them. Read the answers listed; you will find best possible answers along with strategies and suggestions.

1: Tell me about a time when you worked additional hours to finish a project.

Answer:

It's important for your employer to see that you are dedicated to your work, and willing to put in extra hours when required or when a job calls for it. However, be careful when explaining why you were called to work additional hours – for instance, did you have to stay late because you set goals poorly earlier in the process? Or on a more positive note, were you working additional hours because a client requested for a deadline to be moved up on short notice? Stress your competence and willingness to give 110% every time.

2: Tell me about a time when your performance exceeded the duties and requirements of your job.

Answer:

If you're a great candidate for the position, this should be an easy question to answer – choose a time when you truly went above and beyond the call of duty, and put in additional work or voluntarily took on new responsibilities. Remain humble, and express gratitude for the learning opportunity, as well as confidence in your ability to give a repeat performance.

3: What is your driving attitude about work?

Answer:

There are many possible good answers to this question, and the interviewer primarily wants to see that you have a great passion for the job and that you will remain motivated in your career if hired. Some specific driving forces behind your success may include hard work, opportunity, growth potential, or success.

4: Do you take work home with you?

Answer:

It is important to first clarify that you are always willing to take work home when necessary, but you want to emphasize as well that it has not been an issue for you in the past. Highlight skills such as time management, goal-setting, and multi-tasking, which can all ensure that work is completed at work.

5: Describe a typical work day to me.

Answer:

There are several important components in your typical work day, and an interviewer may derive meaning from any or all of them, as well as from your ability to systematically lead him or her through the day. Start at the beginning of your day and proceed chronologically, making sure to emphasize steady productivity, time for review, goal-setting, and prioritizing, as well as some additional time to account for unexpected things that may arise.

6: Tell me about a time when you went out of your way at your previous job.

Answer:

Here it is best to use a specific example of the situation that required you to go out of your way, what your specific position would have required that you did, and how you went above that. Use concrete details, and be sure to include the results, as well as reflection on what you learned in the process.

7: Are you open to receiving feedback and criticisms on your job performance, and adjusting as necessary?

Answer:

This question has a pretty clear answer – yes – but you'll need to display a knowledge as to why this is important. Receiving feedback and criticism is one thing, but the most important part of that process is to then implement it into your daily work. Keep a good attitude, and express that you always appreciate constructive feedback.

8: What inspires you?

Answer:

You may find inspiration in nature, reading success stories, or mastering a difficult task, but it's important that your inspiration is positively-based and that you're able to listen and tune into it when it appears. Keep this answer generally based in the professional world, but where applicable, it may stretch a bit into creative exercises in your personal life that, in turn, help you in achieving career objectives.

9: How do you inspire others?

Answer:

This may be a difficult question, as it is often hard to discern the effects of inspiration in others. Instead of offering a specific example of a time when you inspired someone, focus on general principles such as leading by example that you employ in your professional life. If possible, relate this to a quality that someone who inspired you possessed, and discuss the way you have modified or modelled it in your own work.

10: What has been your biggest success?

Answer:

Your biggest success should be something that was especially meaningful to you, and that you can talk about passionately – your interviewer will be able to see this. Always have an answer prepared for this question, and be sure to explain how you achieved success, as well as what you learned from the experience.

11: What motivates you?

Answer:

It's best to focus on a key aspect of your work that you can target as a "driving force" behind your everyday work. Whether it's customer service, making a difference, or the chance to further your skills and gain experience, it's important that the interviewer can see the passion you hold for your career and the dedication you have to the position.

12: What do you do when you lose motivation?

Answer:

The best candidates will answer that they rarely lose motivation, because they already employ strategies to keep themselves inspired, and because they remain dedicated to their objectives. Additionally, you may impress the interviewer by explaining that you are motivated by achieving goals and advancing, so small successes are always a great way to regain momentum.

13: What do you like to do in your free time?

Answer:

What you do answer here is not nearly as important as what you don't answer – your interviewer does not want to hear that you like to drink, party, or revel in the nightlife. Instead, choose a few activities to focus on that are greater signs of stability and maturity, and that will not detract from your ability to show up to work and be productive, such as reading, cooking, or photography. This is also a great opportunity to show your interviewer that you are a well-rounded, interesting, and dynamic personality that they would be happy to hire.

14: What sets you apart from other workers?

Answer:

This question is a great opportunity to highlight the specific skill sets and passion you bring to the company that no one else can. If you can't outline exactly what sets you apart from other workers, how will the interviewer see it? Be prepared with a thorough outline of what you will bring to the table, in order to help the company achieve their goals.

15: Why are you the best candidate for that position?
Answer:
Have a brief response prepared in advance for this question, as this is another very common theme in interviews (variations of the question include: "Why should I hire you, above Candidate B?" and "What can you bring to our company that Candidate B cannot?"). Make sure that your statement does not sound rehearsed, and highlight your most unique qualities that show the interviewer why he or she must hire you above all the other candidates. Include specific details about your experience and special projects or recognition you've received that set you apart, and show your greatest passion, commitment, and enthusiasm for the position.

16: What does it take to be successful?
Answer:
Hard work, passion, motivation, and a dedication to learning – these are all potential answers to the ambiguous concept of success. It doesn't matter so much which of these values you choose as the primary means to success, or if you choose a combination of them. It is, however, absolutely key that whichever value you choose, you must clearly display in your

attitude, experience, and goals.

17: What would be the biggest challenge in this position for you?

Answer:

Keep this answer positive, and remain focused on the opportunities for growth and learning that the position can provide. Be sure that no matter what the challenge is, it's obvious that you're ready and enthusiastic to tackle it, and that you have a full awareness of what it will take to get the job done.

18: Would you describe yourself as an introvert or an extrovert?

Answer:

There are beneficial qualities to each of these, and your answer may depend on what type of work you're involved in. However, a successful leader may be an introvert or extrovert, and similarly, solid team members may also be either. The important aspect of this question is to have the level of self-awareness required to accurately describe yourself.

19: What are some positive character traits that you don't possess?

Answer:

If an interviewer asks you a tough question about your weaknesses, or lack of positive traits, it's best to keep your answer light-hearted and simple – for instance, express your great confidence in your own abilities, followed by a (rather humble) admittance that you could occasionally do to be more humble.

20: What is the greatest lesson you've ever learned?

Answer:

While this is a very broad question, the interviewer will be more interested in hearing what kind of emphasis you place on this value. Your greatest lesson may tie in with something a mentor, parent, or professor once told you, or you may have gleaned it from a book written by a leading expert in your field. Regardless of what the lesson is, it is most important that you can offer an example of how you've incorporated it into your life.

21: Have you ever been in a situation where one of your strengths became a weakness in an alternate setting?

Answer:

It's important to show an awareness of yourself by having an answer for this question, but you want to make sure that the weakness is relatively minor, and that it would still remain a strength in most settings. For instance, you may be an avid reader who reads anything and everything you can find, but reading billboards while driving to work may be a dangerous idea.

22: Who has been the most influential person in your life?

Answer:

Give a specific example (and name) to the person who has influenced your life greatly, and offer a relevant anecdote about a meaningful exchange the two of you shared. It's great if their influence relates to your professional life, but this particular question opens up the possibility to discuss inspiration in your personal life as well. The interviewer wants to see that you're able to make strong connections with other individuals, and to work under the guiding influence of another person.

23: Do you consider yourself to be a "detailed" or "big picture" type of person?

Answer:

Both of these are great qualities, and it's best if you can incorporate each into your answer. Choose one as your primary type, and relate it to experience or specific items from your resume. Then, explain how the other type fits into your work as well.

24: What is your greatest fear?

Answer:

Disclosing your greatest fear openly and without embarrassment is a great way to show your confidence to an employer. Choose a fear that you are clearly doing work to combat, such as a fear of failure that will seem impossible to the interviewer for someone such as yourself, with such clear goals and actions plans outlined. As tempting as it may be to stick with an easy answer such as spiders, stay away from these, as they don't really tell the interviewer anything about yourself that's relevant.

25: What sort of challenges do you enjoy?

Answer:

The challenges you enjoy should demonstrate some sort of initiative or growth potential on your part, and should also be in line with your career objectives. Employers will evaluate consistency here, as they analyze critically how the challenges you look forward to are related to your ultimate goals.

26: Tell me about a time you were embarrassed. How did you handle it?

Answer:

No one wants to bring up times they were embarrassed in a job interview, and it's probably best to avoid an anecdote here. However, don't shy away from offering a brief synopsis, followed by a display of your ability to laugh it off. Show the interviewer that it was not an event that impacted you significantly.

27: What is your greatest weakness?

Answer:

This is another one of the most popular questions asked in job interviews, so you should be prepared with an answer already. Try to come up with a weakness that you have that can actually be a strength in an alternate setting – such as, "I'm very detail-oriented and like to ensure that things are done correctly, so I sometimes have difficulty in delegating tasks to others." However, don't try to mask obvious weaknesses – if you have little practical experience in the field, mention that you're looking forward to great opportunities to further your knowledge.

28: What are the three best adjectives to describe you in a work setting?

Answer:

While these three adjectives probably already appear somewhere on your resume, don't be afraid to use them again in order to highlight your best qualities. This is a chance for you to sell yourself to the interviewer, and to point out traits you possess that other candidates do not. Use the most specific and accurate words you can think of, and elaborate shortly on how you embody each.

29: What are the three best adjectives to describe you in your personal life?

Answer:

Ideally, the three adjectives that describe you in your personal life should be similar to the adjectives that describe you in your professional life. Employers appreciate consistency, and while they may be understanding of you having an alternate personality outside of the office, it's best if you employ similar principles in your actions both on and off the clock.

30: What type of worker are you?
Answer:

This is an opportunity for you to highlight some of your greatest assets. Characterize some of your talents such as dedicated, self-motivated, detail-oriented, passionate, hard-working, analytical, or customer service focused. Stay away from your weaker qualities here, and remain on the target of all the wonderful things that you can bring to the company.

31: Tell me about your happiest day at work.
Answer:

Your happiest day at work should include one of your greatest professional successes, and how it made you feel. Stay focused on what you accomplished, and be sure to elaborate on how rewarding or satisfying the achievement was for you.

32: Tell me about your worst day at work.
Answer:

It may have been the worst day ever because of all the mistakes you made, or because you'd just had a huge argument with your best friend, but make sure to keep this answer professionally focused. Try to use an example in which something uncontrollable happened in the workplace (such as an important member of a team quit unexpectedly, which ruined your team's meeting with a client), and focus on the frustration of not being in control of the situation. Keep this answer brief, and be sure to end with a reflection on what you learned from the day.

33: What are you passionate about?

Answer:

Keep this answer professionally-focused where possible, but it may also be appropriate to discuss personal issues you are passionate about as well (such as the environment or volunteering at a soup kitchen). Stick to issues that are non-controversial, and allow your passion to shine through as you explain what inspires you about the topic and how you stay actively engaged in it. Additionally, if you choose a personal passion, make sure it is one that does not detract from your availability to work or to be productive.

34: What is the piece of criticism you receive most often?

Answer:

An honest, candid answer to this question can greatly impress an interviewer (when, of course, it is coupled with an explanation of what you're doing to improve), but make sure the criticism is something minimal or unrelated to your career.

35: What type of work environment do you succeed the most in?

Answer:

Be sure to research the company and the specific position before heading into the interview. Tailor your response to fit the job you'd be working in, and explain why you enjoy that type of environment over others. However, it's also extremely important to be adaptable, so remain flexible to other environments as well.

36: Are you an emotional person?

Answer:

It's best to focus on your positive emotions – passion, happiness, motivations – and to stay away from other extreme emotions that may cause you to appear unbalanced. While you want to display your excitement for the job, be sure to remain level-headed and cool at all times, so that the interviewer knows you're not the type of person who lets emotions take you over and get in the way of your work.

37: How do you make decisions?

Answer:

This is a great opportunity for you to wow your interviewer with your decisiveness, confidence, and organizational skills. Make sure that you outline a process for decision-making, and that you stress the importance of weighing your options, as well as in trusting intuition. If you answer this question skilfully and with ease, your interviewer will trust in your capability as a worker.

38: What are the most difficult decisions for you to make?

Answer:

Explain your relationship to decision-making, and a general synopsis of the process you take in making choices. If there is a particular type of decision that you often struggle with, such as those that involve other people, make sure to explain why that type of decision is tough for you, and how you are currently engaged in improving your skills.

39: When making a tough decision, how do you gather information?

Answer:

If you're making a tough choice, it's best to gather information from as many sources as possible. Lead the interviewer through your process of taking information from people in different areas, starting first with advice from experts in your field, feedback from co-workers or other clients, and by looking analytically at your own past experiences.

40: Tell me about a decision you made that did not turn out well.

Answer:

Honesty and transparency are great values that your interviewer will appreciate – outline the choice you made, why you made it, the results of your poor decision – and finally (and most importantly!) what you learned from the decision. Give the interviewer reason to trust that you wouldn't make a decision like that again in the future.

41: Are you able to make decisions quickly?

Answer:

You may be able to make decisions quickly, but be sure to communicate your skill in making sound, thorough decisions as well. Discuss the importance of making a decision quickly, and how you do so, as well as the necessity for each decision to first be well-informed.

42: Tell me about your favorite book or newspaper.

Answer:

The interviewer will look at your answer to this question in order to determine your ability to analyze and review critically. Additionally, try to choose something that is on a topic related to your field or that embodies a theme important to your work, and be able to explain how it relates. Stay away from controversial subject matter, such as politics or religion.

43: If you could be rich or famous, which would you choose?

Answer:

This question speaks to your ability to think creatively, but your answer may also give great insight to your character. If you answer rich, your interviewer may interpret that you are self-confident and don't seek approval from others, and that you like to be rewarded for your work. If you choose famous, your interviewer may gather that you like to be well-known and to deal with people, and to have the platform to deliver your message to others. Either way, it's important to back up your answer with sound reasoning.

44: If you could trade places with anyone for a week, who would it be and why?

Answer:

This question is largely designed to test your ability to think on your feet, and to come up with a reasonable answer to an outside the box question. Whoever you choose, explain your answer in a logical manner, and offer specific professional reasons that led you to choose the individual.

45: What would you say if I told you that just from glancing over your resume, I can already see three spelling mistakes?

Answer:

Clearly, your resume should be absolutely spotless – and you should be confident that it is. If your interviewer tries to make you second-guess yourself here, remain calm and poised and assert with a polite smile that you would be quite surprised as you are positive that your resume is error-free.

46: Tell me about your worldview.

Answer:

This question is designed to offer insight into your personality, so be aware of how the interviewer will interpret your answer. Speak openly and directly, and try to incorporate your own job skills into your outlook on life. For example, discuss your beliefs on the ways that hard work and dedication can always bring success, or in how learning new things is one of life's greatest gifts. It's okay to expand into general life principles here, but try to keep your thoughts related to the professional field as well.

47: What is the biggest mistake someone could make in an interview?

Answer:

The biggest mistake that could be made in an interview is to be caught off guard! Make sure that you don't commit whatever you answer here, and additionally be prepared for all questions. Other common mistakes include asking too early in the hiring process about job benefits, not having questions prepared when the interviewer asks if you have questions, arriving late, dressing casually or sloppily, or showing ignorance of the position.

48: If you won the $50m lottery, what would you do with the money?

Answer:

While a question such as this may seem out of place in a job interview, it's important to display your creative thinking and your ability to think on the spot. It's also helpful if you choose something admirable, yet believable, to do with the money such as donate the first seventy percent to a charitable cause, and divide the remainder among gifts for friends, family, and of course, yourself.

49: Is there ever a time when honesty isn't appropriate in the workplace?

Answer:

This may be a difficult question, but the only time that honesty isn't appropriate in the workplace is perhaps when you're feeling anger or another emotion that is best kept to yourself. If this is the case, explain simply that it is best to put some thoughts aside, and clarify that the process of keeping some thoughts quiet is often enough to smooth over any unsettled emotions, thus eliminating the problem.

50: If you could travel anywhere in the world, where would it be?

Answer:

This question is meant to allow you to be creative – so go ahead and stretch your thoughts to come up with a unique answer. However, be sure to keep your answer professionally-minded. For example, choose somewhere rich with culture or that would expose you to a new experience, rather than going on an expensive cruise through the Bahamas.

51: What would I find in your refrigerator right now?

Answer:

An interviewer may ask a creative question such as this in

order to discern your ability to answer unexpected questions calmly, or, to try to gain some insight into your personality. For example, candidates with a refrigerator full of junk food or take-out may be more likely to be under stress or have health issues, while a candidate with a balanced refrigerator full of nutritious staples may be more likely to lead a balanced mental life, as well.

52: If you could play any sport professionally, what would it be and what aspect draws you to it?

Answer:

Even if you don't know much about professional sports, this question might be a great opportunity to highlight some of your greatest professional working skills. For example, you may choose to play professional basketball, because you admire the teamwork and coordination that goes into creating a solid play. Or, you may choose to play professional tennis, because you consider yourself to be a go-getter with a solid work ethic and great dedication to perfecting your craft. Explain your choice simply to the interviewer without elaborating on drawn-out sports metaphors, and be sure to point out specific areas or skills in which you excel.

53 Who were the presidential and vice-presidential candidates in the 2008 elections?

Answer:

This question, plain and simple, is intended as a gauge of your intelligence and awareness. If you miss this question, you may well fail the interview. Offer your response with a polite smile, because you understand that there are some individuals who probably miss this question.

54: Explain X task in a few short sentences as you would to a second-grader.

Answer:

An interviewer may ask you to break down a normal job task that you would complete in a manner that a child could understand, in part to test your knowledge of the task's inner workings – but in larger part, to test your ability to explain a process in simple, basic terms. While you and your co-workers may be able to converse using highly technical language, being able to simplify a process is an important skill for any employee to have.

55: If you could compare yourself to any animal, what would it be?

Answer:

Many interviewers ask this question, and it's not to determine which character traits you think you embody – instead, the interviewer wants to see that you can think outside the box, and that you're able to reason your way through any situation. Regardless of what animal you answer, be sure that you provide a thorough reason for your choice.

56: Who is your hero?

Answer:

Your hero may be your mother or father, an old professor, someone successful in your field, or perhaps even Wonder Woman – but keep your reasoning for your choice professional, and be prepared to offer a logical train of thought. Choose someone who embodies values that are important in your chosen career field, and answer the question with a smile and sense of passion.

57: Who would play you in the movie about your life?

Answer:

As with many creative questions that challenge an interviewee to think outside the box, the answer to this question is not as important as how you answer it. Choose a professional, and relatively non-controversial actor or actress, and then be prepared to offer specific reasoning for your choice, employing important skills or traits you possess.

58: Name five people, alive or dead, that would be at your ideal dinner party.

Answer:

Smile and sound excited at the opportunity to think outside the box when asked this question, even if it seems to come from left field. Choose dynamic, inspiring individuals who you could truly learn from, and explain what each of them would have to offer to the conversation. Don't forget to include yourself, and to talk about what you would bring to the conversation as well!

59: What is customer service?

Answer:

Customer service can be many things – and the most important consideration in this question is that you have a creative answer. Demonstrate your ability to think outside the box by offering a confident answer that goes past a basic definition, and that shows you have truly considered your own individual view of what it means to take care of your customers. The thoughtful consideration you hold for customers will speak for itself.

60: Tell me about a time when you went out of your way for a customer.

Answer:

It's important that you offer an example of a time you truly went out of your way – be careful not to confuse something that felt like a big effort on your part, with something your employer would expect you to do anyway. Offer an example of the customer's problems, what you did to solve it, and the way the customer responded after you took care of the situation.

61: How do you gain confidence from customers?

Answer:

This is a very open-ended question that allows you to show your customer service skills to the interviewer. There are many possible answers, and it is best to choose something that you've had great experience with, such as "by handling situations with transparency," "offering rewards," or "focusing on great communication." Offer specific examples of successes you've had.

62: Tell me about a time when a customer was upset or agitated – how did you handle the situation?

Answer:

Similarly to handling a dispute with another employee, the most important part to answering this question is to first set up the scenario, offer a step-by-step guide to your particular conflict resolution style, and end by describing the way the conflict was resolved. Be sure that in answering questions about your own conflict resolution style, that you emphasize the importance of open communication and understanding from both parties, as well as a willingness to reach a compromise or other solution.

63: When can you make an exception for a customer?

Answer:

Exceptions for customers can generally be made when in accordance with company policy or when directed by a supervisor. Display an understanding of the types of situations in which an exception should be considered, such as when a customer has endured a particular hardship, had a complication with an order, or at a request.

64: What would you do in a situation where you were needed by both a customer and your boss?

Answer:

While both your customer and your boss have different needs of you and are very important to your success as a worker, it is always best to try to attend to your customer first – however, the key is explaining to your boss why you are needed urgently by the customer, and then to assure your boss that you will attend to his or her needs as soon as possible (unless it's absolutely an urgent matter).

65: What is the most important aspect of customer service?

Answer:

While many people would simply state that customer satisfaction is the most important aspect of customer service, it's important to be able to elaborate on other important techniques in customer service situations. Explain why customer service is such a key part of business, and be sure to expand on the aspect that you deem to be the most important in a way that is reasoned and well-thought out.

66: Is it best to create low or high expectations for a customer?

Answer:

You may answer this question either way (after, of course, determining that the company does not have a clear opinion on the matter). However, no matter which way you answer the question, you must display a thorough thought process, and very clear reasoning for the option you chose. Offer pros and cons of each, and include the ultimate point that tips the scale in favor of your chosen answer.

67: Why would your skills be a good match with X objective of our company?

Answer:

If you've researched the company before the interview, answering this question should be no problem. Determine several of the company's main objectives, and explain how specific skills that you have are conducive to them. Also, think about ways that your experience and skills can translate to helping the company expand upon these objectives, and to reach further goals. If your old company had a similar objective, give a specific example of how you helped the company to meet it.

68: What do you think this job entails?

Answer:

Make sure you've researched the position well before heading into the interview. Read any and all job descriptions you can find (at best, directly from the employer's website or job posting), and make note of key duties, responsibilities, and experience required. Few things are less impressive to an interviewer than a candidate who has no idea what sort of job they're actually being interviewed for.

69: Is there anything else about the job or company you'd like to know?

Answer:

If you have learned about the company beforehand, this is a great opportunity to show that you put in the effort to study before the interview. Ask questions about the company's mission in relation to current industry trends, and engage the interviewer in interesting, relevant conversation. Additionally, clear up anything else you need to know about the specific position before leaving – so that if the interviewer calls with an offer, you'll be prepared to answer.

70: Are you the best candidate for this position?

Answer:

Yes! Offer specific details about what makes you qualified for this position, and be sure to discuss (and show) your unbridled passion and enthusiasm for the new opportunity, the job, and the company.

71: How did you prepare for this interview?

Answer:

The key part of this question is to make sure that you have

prepared! Be sure that you've researched the company, their objectives, and their services prior to the interview, and know as much about the specific position as you possibly can. It's also helpful to learn about the company's history and key players in the current organization.

72: If you were hired here, what would you do on your first day?

Answer:

While many people will answer this question in a boring fashion, going through the standard first day procedures, this question is actually a great chance for you to show the interviewer why you will make a great hire. In addition to things like going through training or orientation, emphasize how much you would enjoy meeting your supervisors and co-workers, or how you would spend a lot of the day asking questions and taking in all of your new surroundings.

73: Have you viewed our company's website?

Answer:

Clearly, you should have viewed the company's website and done some preliminary research on them before coming to the interview. If for some reason you did not, do not say that you did, as the interviewer may reveal you by asking a specific question about it. If you did look at the company's website, this is an appropriate time to bring up something you saw there that was of particular interest to you, or a value that you especially supported.

74: How does X experience on your resume relate to this position?

Answer:

Many applicants will have some bit of experience on their resume that does not clearly translate to the specific job in question. However, be prepared to be asked about this type of seemingly-irrelevant experience, and have a response prepared that takes into account similar skill sets or training that the two may share.

75: Why do you want this position?

Answer:

Keep this answer focused positively on aspects of this specific job that will allow you to further your skills, offer new experience, or that will be an opportunity for you to do something that you particularly enjoy. Don't tell the interviewer that you've been looking for a job for a long time, or that the pay is very appealing, or you will appear unmotivated and opportunistic.

76 How is your background relevant to this position?

Answer:

Ideally, this should be obvious from your resume. However, in instances where your experience is more loosely-related to the position, make sure that you've researched the job and company well before the interview. That way, you can intelligently relate the experience and skills that you do have, to similar skills that would be needed in the new position. Explain specifically how your skills will translate, and use words to describe your background such as "preparation" and "learning." Your prospective position should be described as an "opportunity" and a chance for "growth and development."

77: How do you feel about X mission of our company?
Answer:

It's important to have researched the company prior to the interview – and if you've done so, this question won't catch you off guard. The best answer is one that is simple, to the point, and shows knowledge of the mission at hand. Offer a few short statements as to why you believe in the mission's importance, and note that you would be interested in the chance to work with a company that supports it.

INDEX

Data Structures and Algorithms Interview Questions

Data Structures
Genaral Concepts of Data Structures

Arrays

Stacks

Queues

Lists

51: How to insert into a doubly linked list?

52: Write a C program to insert into a circular singly linked list

53: Explain traversing through a linked list.

54: What are the differences between a linked list and an array?

55: Consider a linked list with the following data:

Hash Data structures

56: What is a hashing?

57: What is a hash table?

58: What is linear probing?

59: What are the common uses of hash tables?

60: How do you use the right hash function?

61: Explain Collision resolution.

62: Explain Chaining.

63: Explain Open addressing.

64: What are the differences between Chaining and Open Addressing?

65: What are the problems with hash tables?

66: Explain Probabilistic hashing.

67: Explain Perfect hashing.

68: Explain Coalesced hashing.

69: Explain Extendible hashing.

70: Explain Linear hashing.

Trees

71: Explain the Tree data structure.

72: What are the properties of a tree?

73: Explain Node, Edge, Leaf, and Root of a tree.

74: Differentiate among Parent, Sibling and Subtree of a tree.

75: What is a red-black tree?

76: Explain Tree Traversal.

77: Explain Preorder.

78: Explain Postorder.

79: Explain Inorder.

Sets

Graphs

109: What is a Graph data structure?

110: What is the difference between Graph and a Tree data structure?

111: Explain Vertex, Edge, Adjacency and Path in a Graph

112: What are the different types of Graphs?

113: Explain Graph representations.

114: What are the basic operations in a Graph?

115: Explain the IsReachable function implementation.

116: Explain Graph traversals.

117: Explain DFS in Graph.

118: Explain BFS in Graph.

119: Explain some of the common applications of Graph.

120: How do you represent a graph using a matrix?

121: Explain Adjacency Matrix

122: What are the advantages and disadvantages of Adjacency Matrix?

123: Explain Adjacency List.

124: What are the advantages and disadvantages of Adjacency List?

125: What do you mean by cost of a graph?

126: Explain the Minimum Spanning Tree problem.

127: How are Graphs advantageous in implementing real-time solutions?

128: What is Incidence matrix?

129: What is Incidence list?

130: How do you find the shortest path in a Graph?

Algorithms
General Concepts of Algorithms

131: What do you mean by Algorithm?

132: What are input specialized and strategy specialized algorithms?

133: What are the different types of input specialized Algorithms commonly used?

134: What are the different Strategy specialized algorithms?

135: Explain Divide-and-Conquer Algorithm.

136: Give some examples of Divide-and-Conquer Algorithm.

Sorting Algorithms

168: Explain Bucket sort.

169: Explain Radix sort.

170: What do you mean by index sorting?

171: Explain Pigeonhole Sort.

172: Explain some of the issues faced for implementation of quicksort.

173: What do you mean by shuffling?

174: Explain Cycle Sort.

175: Explain sorted insert into a singly linked list.

176: Which algorithms takes minimum number of memory writes and why?

177: Why is quick sort preferred for Arrays and merge sort for Linked lists?

Search Algorithms

178: Explain the algorithm for linear search.

179: Explain the algorithm for binary search.

180: Explain interpolation search.

181: Write the algorithm to find the largest element in an array of unique elements .

182: Write the algorithm to find the LCM of array elements.

183: Write the algorithm to find the position of an element in the given sorted array of infinite elements.

184: Write the algorithm to find how many times an element repeats in a sorted array.

185: Explain the Graph BFS Algorithm.

186: Explain the Graph DFS Algorithm.

187: Write the algorithm to check if the given array is a subset of another array, using Binary Search.

188: How will you search in an almost sorted array?

189: Explain why a Binary search is better than a Ternary search.

190: How can we check if the given tree is a binary heap?

Huffman Coding

191: What is Huffman Coding?

192: How do you generate a Huffman Tree from a given set of values?

HR Questions

1: Tell me about a time when you worked additional hours to finish a project.

2: Tell me about a time when your performance exceeded the duties and requirements of your job.

3: What is your driving attitude about work?

4: Do you take work home with you?

5: Describe a typical work day to me.

6: Tell me about a time when you went out of your way at your previous job.

7: Are you open to receiving feedback and criticisms on your job performance, and adjusting as necessary?

8: What inspires you?

9: How do you inspire others?

10: What has been your biggest success?

11: What motivates you?

12: What do you do when you lose motivation?

13: What do you like to do in your free time?

14: What sets you apart from other workers?

15: Why are you the best candidate for that position?

16: What does it take to be successful?

17: What would be the biggest challenge in this position for you?

18: Would you describe yourself as an introvert or an extrovert?

19: What are some positive character traits that you don't possess?

20: What is the greatest lesson you've ever learned?

21: Have you ever been in a situation where one of your strengths became a weakness in an alternate setting?

22: Who has been the most influential person in your life?

23: Do you consider yourself to be a "detailed" or "big picture" type of person?

24: What is your greatest fear?

25: What sort of challenges do you enjoy?

26: Tell me about a time you were embarrassed. How did you handle it?

27: What is your greatest weakness?

28: What are the three best adjectives to describe you in a work setting?

58: Name five people, alive or dead, that would be at your ideal dinner party.

59: What is customer service?

60: Tell me about a time when you went out of your way for a customer.

61: How do you gain confidence from customers?

62: Tell me about a time when a customer was upset or agitated – how did you handle the situation?

63: When can you make an exception for a customer?

64: What would you do in a situation where you were needed by both a customer and your boss?

65: What is the most important aspect of customer service?

66: Is it best to create low or high expectations for a customer?

67: Why would your skills be a good match with X objective of our company?

68: What do you think this job entails?

69: Is there anything else about the job or company you'd like to know?

70: Are you the best candidate for this position?

71: How did you prepare for this interview?

72: If you were hired here, what would you do on your first day?

73: Have you viewed our company's website?

74: How does X experience on your resume relate to this position?

75: Why do you want this position?

76 How is your background relevant to this position?

77: How do you feel about X mission of our company?

Some of the following titles might also be handy:

1. .NET Interview Questions You'll Most Likely Be Asked
2. 200 Interview Questions You'll Most Likely Be Asked
3. Access VBA Programming Interview Questions You'll Most Likely Be Asked
4. Adobe ColdFusion Interview Questions You'll Most Likely Be Asked
5. Advanced Excel Interview Questions You'll Most Likely Be Asked
6. Advanced JAVA Interview Questions You'll Most Likely Be Asked
7. Advanced SAS Interview Questions You'll Most Likely Be Asked
8. AJAX Interview Questions You'll Most Likely Be Asked
9. Algorithms Interview Questions You'll Most Likely Be Asked
10. Android Development Interview Questions You'll Most Likely Be Asked
11. Ant & Maven Interview Questions You'll Most Likely Be Asked
12. Apache Web Server Interview Questions You'll Most Likely Be Asked
13. Artificial Intelligence Interview Questions You'll Most Likely Be Asked
14. ASP.NET Interview Questions You'll Most Likely Be Asked
15. Automated Software Testing Interview Questions You'll Most Likely Be Asked
16. Base SAS Interview Questions You'll Most Likely Be Asked
17. BEA WebLogic Server Interview Questions You'll Most Likely Be Asked
18. C & C++ Interview Questions You'll Most Likely Be Asked
19. C# Interview Questions You'll Most Likely Be Asked
20. C++ Internals Interview Questions You'll Most Likely Be Asked
21. CCNA Interview Questions You'll Most Likely Be Asked
22. Cloud Computing Interview Questions You'll Most Likely Be Asked
23. Computer Architecture Interview Questions You'll Most Likely Be Asked
24. Computer Networks Interview Questions You'll Most Likely Be Asked
25. Core JAVA Interview Questions You'll Most Likely Be Asked
26. Data Structures & Algorithms Interview Questions You'll Most Likely Be Asked
27. Data WareHousing Interview Questions You'll Most Likely Be Asked
28. EJB 3.0 Interview Questions You'll Most Likely Be Asked
29. Entity Framework Interview Questions You'll Most Likely Be Asked
30. Fedora & RHEL Interview Questions You'll Most Likely Be Asked
31. GNU Development Interview Questions You'll Most Likely Be Asked
32. Hibernate, Spring & Struts Interview Questions You'll Most Likely Be Asked
33. HTML, XHTML and CSS Interview Questions You'll Most Likely Be Asked
34. HTML5 Interview Questions You'll Most Likely Be Asked
35. IBM WebSphere Application Server Interview Questions You'll Most Likely Be Asked
36. iOS SDK Interview Questions You'll Most Likely Be Asked
37. Java / J2EE Design Patterns Interview Questions You'll Most Likely Be Asked
38. Java / J2EE Interview Questions You'll Most Likely Be Asked
39. Java Messaging Service Interview Questions You'll Most Likely Be Asked
40. JavaScript Interview Questions You'll Most Likely Be Asked
41. JavaServer Faces Interview Questions You'll Most Likely Be Asked
42. JDBC Interview Questions You'll Most Likely Be Asked
43. jQuery Interview Questions You'll Most Likely Be Asked
44. JSP-Servlet Interview Questions You'll Most Likely Be Asked
45. JUnit Interview Questions You'll Most Likely Be Asked
46. Linux Commands Interview Questions You'll Most Likely Be Asked
47. Linux Interview Questions You'll Most Likely Be Asked
48. Linux System Administrator Interview Questions You'll Most Likely Be Asked
49. Mac OS X Lion Interview Questions You'll Most Likely Be Asked
50. Mac OS X Snow Leopard Interview Questions You'll Most Likely Be Asked

For complete list visit

www.vibrantpublishers.com

Made in the USA
Las Vegas, NV
11 March 2022

45471782R00118